HOME

Executive Editor
CLAY IDE

Style Consultant
PATRICK PRINTY

Editor
SAMANTHA MOSS

BONNIER BOOKS

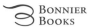

BONNIER BOOKS

This edition published by Bonnier Books,
Appledram Barns, Birdham Road, Chichester,
West Sussex PO20 7EQ, UK
Bonnier Books Web site:
www.bonnierbooks.co.uk

WELDON OWEN PUBLISHING
Chief Executive Officer John Owen

WELDON OWEN
Chief Operating Officer, President Terry Newell
Vice President, Publisher Roger Shaw
Vice President, Creative Director Gaye Allen
Vice President, International Sales Stuart Laurence

Senior Art Director Emma Boys
Associate Publisher Katherine Pearson
Managing Editor Laurie Wertz
Contributing Editor Peter Cieply
Designers Shadin Saah, Briar Levit

Production Director Chris Hemesath
Colour Manager Teri Bell
Photo Co-ordinator Meghan Hildebrand
UK Translation Grant Laing Partnership

Set in Bembo™ and Agenda™

Colour separations by Mission Productions Limited, Hong Kong
Printed in Singapore by Tien Wah Press (Pte.) Ltd.

10 9 8 7 6 5 4 3 2 1

ISBN 978-1-905825-18-9

A Welcoming Home

It's been said that a person's home tells more about them than words ever could. Maybe that's because our homes allow us the unique freedom to surround ourselves with our favourite colours, textures, objects, and memories.

Over the last few decades, the shift to a more casual lifestyle has changed the way we inhabit our homes. Formally defined rooms, each once reserved for a single activity, have given way to versatile spaces that flow easily into one another. New advances in weather-resistant materials have extended living spaces outdoors, with decks, verandas, and patios being furnished with the same comfort and style as the living room. Bathrooms have become larger, with greater emphasis on creating a spa experience. Telecommuting has made home offices more common, and affordable new entertainment technology has led to an increasing presence of media rooms in our floor plans. In the midst of all these changes, however, one truth remains the same: people are passionate about their homes.

We created this book to address the challenges we all face when we decorate our homes. The following pages include floor plans, colour charts, a materials guide, and hundreds of simple style ideas that will help make decorating your home as easy, fun, and inspiring as it's supposed to be. In the interest of simplicity, we've divided the book into chapters by rooms and activities. We hope you'll discover, however, that a truly beautiful home is much more than a series of rooms. It's the ultimate expression of you and your family.

Contents

YOUR HOME

"MY HOME IS A

VIVID REFLECTION OF

WHO I AM. IT SURROUNDS

ME WITH THE THINGS

I LOVE MOST, AND SETS

THE SCENE FOR NEW

MEMORIES TO BE MADE."

For most of us, "living well" begins and ends with the private world we create for ourselves and share with friends. The homes we live in today are different in many ways from the homes we grew up in. Over the years there's been a shift away from formality and a greater emphasis on individuality, personal expression, and casual style. Gilding and grandeur are fine if you want them, and room can always be found for a fine antique, but the greatest luxury in contemporary life is

MAKING YOUR HOUSE
YOUR HOME

CREATING A COMFORTABLE, WELCOMING HOME THAT REFLECTS YOUR UNIQUE CHARACTER IS ONE OF LIFE'S GREATEST PLEASURES – AND ONE OF ITS GREATEST REWARDS.

without a doubt comfort – in all its guises, and in abundance. Before we can call a house a home, it must be as welcoming and soothing as it is beautiful. After all, your end goal is not merely having a striking new sofa and wall colour for the living room; it is also knowing that everyone feels at home in the room. The basic elements of an appealing room are easy to identify: comfortable, well-designed seating that encourages conversation; harmony of colour; lighting that meets your needs and influences your mood; beautiful things to admire and touch; and an overall sense of ease. These fundamentals of comfort remain the same throughout the entire house, from luxurious master bathrooms or state-of-the-art home offices to well-appointed outdoor rooms. How these individual elements come together – the mix of furniture and accessories, the contrasts of texture, the use of colour, the unexpected objects that give a home its character – is up to you to decide. Style depends neither on a single choice nor on a fixed set of rules; it is instead about creating a successful marriage of beauty and comfort.

Style is shaped by the way you and your family live. It is the sum of a room's many parts and possibilities, arranged to tell a distinctive, coherent story. In this book you'll find creative decorating ideas that will help you weave your own story through every area of your home. If you work with an experienced interior designer, you can go far in breaking the rules and daring to take risks. But you don't need professional advice to create a comfortable home. You just need to

DECORATING IS NOT ABOUT IMITATING A STYLE. IT'S ABOUT EXPRESSING YOUR OWN.

know what you love, and trust your preferences to guide you. The simplest route to identifying your style is to spend time leafing through design magazines, books, and catalogues. Take note of anything that strikes you, whether it's an entire room or just an idea for a window treatment. Clip out photos that have colours, patterns, or shapes that attract you. These clippings may also be based on intangible elements – a quality of light, the size or shape of a room, a warm mood, or the memories evoked by an image. In addition to photo clippings, gather paint and fabric swatches that you like. Start a clippings folder for reference, and continue adding to it until you have three or four dozen entries. Then spread out the collection and see what's there. Is it full of warm wood or stainless steel? Do the rooms burst with colour, or are you naturally drawn to off-white? Are there more sparsely furnished open spaces, or are they mostly intimate rooms filled with

TRUE LUXURY IS ABOUT COMFORT, AND MAKING PEOPLE FEEL AT HOME.

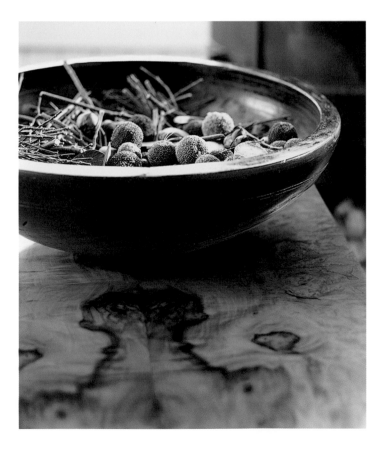

collectables? You'll begin to see a pattern in your choices and end up with a better sense of your innate decorating preferences. All that's necessary now is to make it happen, within budget and in your space.

Whether decorating a small flat or a ten-room house, it's best to begin with an overall colour palette that will be carried out in paint, fabrics, and furnishings and convey a style consistently throughout your home. Decorating is an ongoing, long-term process, so it's best to have something of a master plan in place, so that adjacent rooms flow smoothly from one to another. Thinking in terms of the whole house needn't be seen as restrictive, however. You can still experiment with moods – more formal in some spaces, more playful in

others. Even if you modify it later on, deciding on a colour scheme for the entire house is especially helpful in this early planning stage. It will direct your efforts and spare your having to choose from among too many options. In the Colour chapter of this book (page 302), you'll discover strategies for selecting a palette and making sure it extends harmoniously into all the areas of your home. Once you have your style and colour preferences in mind, tackle one room at a time. If you concentrate on a single space, your efforts will pay off more quickly, and the results will be far more satisfying than if you take on too much simultaneously. This one-step-at-a-time principle also allows you to refine your style choices as you see each room take shape.

SHARING OBJECTS AND MEMORIES THAT ARE IMPORTANT TO YOU IS THE MOST NATURAL EXPRESSION OF YOUR STYLE.

When you've chosen the space that you want to work on, sketch out a floor plan to get your ideas on paper. Throughout this book you'll find practical ideas for mapping out effective floor plans and bringing together all the varied elements that comprise a successful space. Start by establishing seating groups for conversation and areas for activities such as office work or watching films. Look at the traffic patterns through the room and arrange furniture to accommodate smooth passage. Make a list of your lighting needs for the space and make note of possible sources of ambient, accent, and task lighting. Now is the time to consider window treatments, too, whether casual or formal, simple blinds or plush curtains. Then, with your floor plan sketched out, fill in the details by choosing furnishings and

YOUR HOME IS AN ORGANIC, LIVING ENTITY. IT GROWS AND CHANGES JUST AS YOU DO.

accessories with an eye towards your overall style and colour palette. Strive for a balance between long-term investment and affordable splurges. Part of the fun of decorating is playing with the season's new colours or trendy new patterns, but you can enjoy them in a cushion, a throw, or some other accessory instead of committing to them in a major piece of furniture. This approach satisfies a yen for something fresh while preserving a background of choices you can live with

for a long time. When investing in significant pieces, make quality, comfort, and enduring style your guides. Design trends come and go, and homes evolve over time. What remains constant is the need for comfort and the natural desire to put people at ease. Remember that what you are creating is not a showcase but a home that suits the way you live. Making your guests feel at home is less about the design of the chairs and more about the warmth of your welcome.

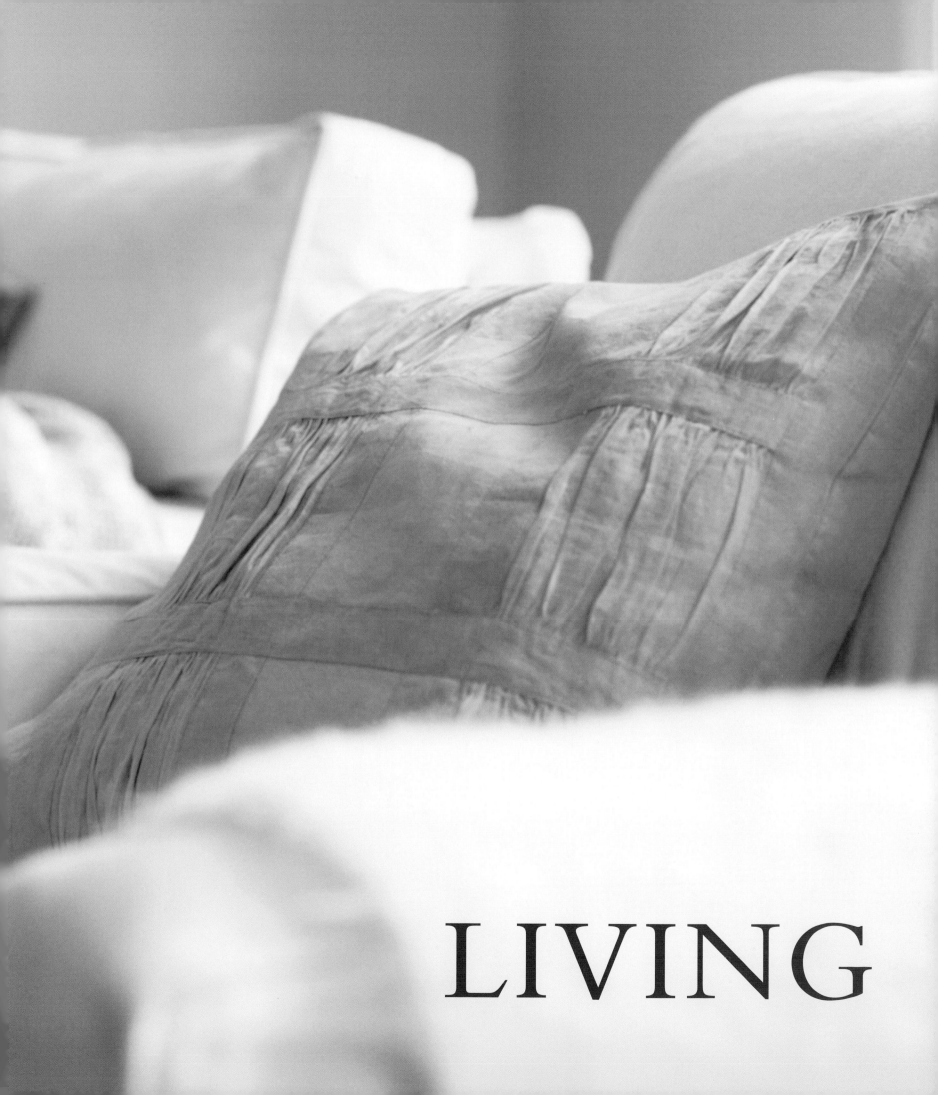

LIVING

"I WANT A ROOM FOR LIVING, A SPACE THAT REFLECTS MY STYLE AND EXPERIENCES, WHERE EVERYONE FEELS COMFORTABLE – AND THEY NEVER WANT TO LEAVE."

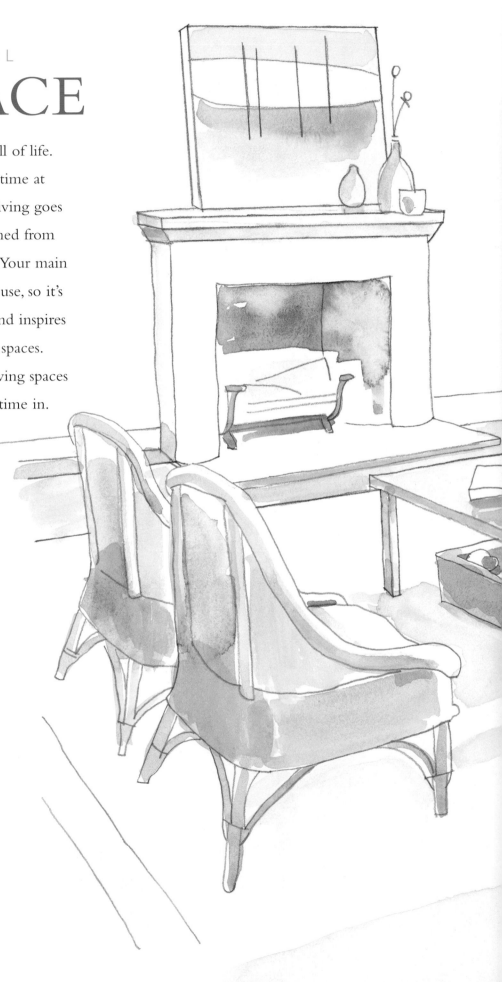

ELEMENTS OF A SUCCESSFUL
LIVING SPACE

Living rooms are, simply put, just that – spaces full of life.
They're the places where we spend much of our time at
home – and a lot of our decorating energy. But living goes
on throughout the whole house, and lessons learned from
the living room apply to every area of the home. Your main
living space in many ways sets a tone for your house, so it's
important to give thought to how it influences and inspires
the decor of adjoining rooms, including outdoor spaces.
In this chapter you'll find ideas that help make living spaces
all through the house more pleasurable to spend time in.

How to Plan a Living Space

The ultimate success of decorating any room depends upon clearly identifying your goals for the space as you begin. In your early planning, focus on functionality as well as style to arrive at an ideal arrangement.

Whether you're redecorating or simply rearranging and refreshing a room, before you start choosing colours and buying new furnishings, take time to map out the room as a whole. Draw a floor plan in a consistent scale and add furnishings in the same scale. Begin by sketching in large furnishings such as sofas, easy chairs, and cupboards on your diagram. These key pieces will determine what other furnishings are needed and how you might use pieces you already have. Then, plan for traffic patterns around them. Major pathways require

90–120 cm (36–48 in) for comfortable passage. Allow at least 45 cm (18 in) between a coffee table and sofa, and 60 cm (24 in) between other pieces of furniture.

Ask yourself how the room will be used, and which additional furnishings are needed – occasional tables, ottomans, lamps, storage pieces, extra chairs, and so on. Do you want the room to be more formal or casual? Will your family use it mostly as a media centre, or do you enjoy entertaining and need multiple conversation areas? Consider adding furnishings that increase the functionality of the space, such as wall shelving for storage or a table that doubles as a bar during parties. Plan for rugs after all furnishings are in place. To anchor a seating group, a rug should be large enough for all the furniture to sit on it. If that's not possible, use a rug slightly larger than the coffee table.

OPEN-PLAN LIVING AREA

This open-plan room (above and preceding page) has separate activity zones that are subtly differentiated while leaving ample space for traffic flow.

■ **A U-SHAPED SEATING GROUP** allows the greatest number of people to sit together.

■ **A DIVIDING LINE** between seating area and dining table is delineated by the back of the sofa.

■ **THE CONVERSATION AREA** is further defined by a large rug, while wood floors in the dining area are left bare.

■ **OPEN PASSAGES** to other rooms and to the outdoor deck are created by "floating" furniture – positioning it away from the walls – in the centre of both spaces.

■ **SMALLER OCCASIONAL CHAIRS** used in the space offer flexibility.

A pair of sideboards adds a sense of architectural detail and provides storage. Lamps on top of each sideboard supplement overhead light and may be dimmed for dining.

KITCHEN

ENTRANCE

A conversation area is set up around the fireplace. Slipper chairs on castors are easily moved to the other areas.

BEDROOMS

Keeping seating generally low – using an armless sectional unit and an ottoman – makes the room appear larger.

L-SHAPED SPACE

This L-shaped space encompasses three different activity zones – for TV watching, conversation, and dining. While each area functions independently, the areas are also designed with an eye towards enhancing the space as a whole.

A rug helps to distinguish the media area, and it is pulled to one side of the entrance to define a "hallway" to the other areas.

A sideboard conceals audio-visual equipment and acts as a focus for the library–media area.

STANDARD SOFA SHAPES

Whatever their shape, the best sofas allow you to change a room's look with a quick switch of accents. Opt for a neutral colour palette, and always place comfort first when selecting a style.

Classic Sofas
Enduring styles avoid trendy designs, which allow sofas to be enjoyed for decades as key furnishings.

Antique-Style Sofas
These have vintage appeal, but cushionless backs are generally not as comfortable as the plump cushion-back models available today.

Sectional Seating
Modular units are a flexible option. As your space changes, add, subtract, or rearrange sections as needed or desired.

Love Seats and Settees
Smaller pieces are a smart solution when space is tight; also consider using them in a large hallway or a bedroom.

ENTRANCE

A pair of lightweight chairs are easy to move when entertaining.

From the entrance, traffic flows around the centre love seat.

A dining-size table behind one love seat serves as a library table for display and may be used for impromptu meals overlooking the fire.

A small writing table can be set up as a bar for parties.

KITCHEN

PLAN FOR ENTERTAINING

If your living room is often the centre of entertaining, supplement sofas with lightweight chairs that can be easily moved around, and provide tables for guests to set food and drinks on.

Decorative lamps (indicated by circles on tables and floor) form a triangle of soft light for evening.

Matching love seats are arranged in a right-angle configuration to create two conversation areas during a larger party.

A room-size carpet should come to within 45–60 cm (18–24 in) of the walls. Furniture along the edges may sit partially off the carpet.

Bringing together friends and family is one of life's greatest joys and privileges. Whether gathering all your loved ones or mixing old friends with new, everyone should always feel at home in your living room. Seating arrangements are the starting point. How you set up a room affects the way that people interact, so plan ahead for gatherings large and small by ensuring that there's plenty of opportunity to mingle. It's true that strangers sometimes find one another across a crowded room, but

GATHERING
FAMILY AND FRIENDS

SUCCESSFUL LIVING SPACES PUT EVERYONE AT EASE, STARTING WITH AN EFFECTIVE SEATING PLAN THAT INSPIRES SPONTANEITY AND INVITES EASY CONVERSATION.

most of us are more comfortable at closer range. Eye contact is key, and it should be easy to establish, whether between an intimate pairing of chairs or within a large conversation circle. Seating configurations require a logic to them, so look for a natural point of focus to provide it. If your room has a fireplace, take advantage of it and arrange a seating group around it during the cool season; a bank of windows looking out at a garden or a water view makes a perfect focal point in the summer. Make sure there's room to bring in extra seating when needed, plenty of places to set down drinks, and lots of cushions for added comfort.

Room for Entertaining

In a space frequently used for parties, multiple seating arrangements in separate areas offer plenty of room for people to mix and mingle.

Successful entertaining is enhanced by a floor plan that eases traffic flow. Where space allows, subdivide seating areas in a large room to form smaller, more intimate groupings. This gives guests a choice of conversations to join, and lets family members use the space simultaneously for different purposes. Before a party, move non-essential pieces out of the way to give a room a more spacious feeling. Then, include lightweight, portable chairs in your seating plan to accommodate more guests and make it easier to move freely from one group to another. In smaller rooms, bring in stackable stools or floor cushions to supplement seating.

WHY THIS ROOM WORKS

Creating three distinct areas for gatherings in this spacious living room makes it perfect for day-to-day family use as well as for entertaining a crowd.

■ **AN OPEN FLOOR PLAN** is inviting to large groups and encourages guests to mingle and interact.

■ **MULTIPLE SEATING AREAS** expand the possibilities for conversation. Two facing sofas flank the fireplace, four easy chairs encircle a coffee table, and a sheltered day-bed provides a spot for a quiet chat.

■ **WHITE UPHOLSTERY** ties the different areas of the room together and creates a mood of serenity.

■ **CASUAL WOODEN CHAIRS** in singular shapes add interest and are easy for guests to move as they please.

■ **RUGS** in a neutral colour anchor the main seating groups without disrupting the unifying effect of the honey-coloured pine flooring.

This room takes a traditional arrangement and gives it a casual update by incorporating informal fabrics and accent pieces.

- **WELL-LOVED ANTIQUES** that show a little character pair with white canvas loose covers for a casual mix.

- **CRISP WHITE TRIM**, on the mantel and French windows, emphasizes the room's architectural details. The collection of vases on the mantel maintains the simplicity of the palette.

- **SOOTHING BLUE WALLS** have classic appeal. The colour is repeated in subtle shadings throughout the space.

- **UNADORNED WINDOWS** allow sunlight to stream through the French windows, and mirrors and silvered surfaces reflect it, adding understated brilliance.

GATHERING FAMILY AND FRIENDS

Classic Comfort

Enliven a traditional room with a mix of vintage and current styles, adding thoughtful accents that place comfort before formality.

The standard seating arrangement of sofa, coffee table, and a pair of chairs all grouped around a fireplace has held its popularity for good reason. It makes great use of space, puts people at ease, and can be rendered with an almost infinite selection of styles. Creative choices in colour, furniture, and accessories allow you to follow a classic decorative framework but bring it up to date, making even the most traditional rooms come alive with a fresh blend of old and new.

To bring a more informal feeling to a traditionally arranged room, begin with seating that feels as good as it looks, upholstered in easy-care fabrics and accented with scatter cushions. Include beautifully weathered or vintage-style pieces to give the room a lived-in look. Use lighter, more casual window treatments – cotton blinds or sailcloth panels instead of heavy curtains, for example – or, leave windows bare or dress them with sheer curtains to establish a bright, airy feeling.

Flexible Seating

When selecting furniture for your living area, choose pieces and arrangements that can be shifted with the seasons or reconfigured for special events. Sectional seating is ideal for this purpose, but you can apply the same principles to other furniture. If you have a pair of sofas, smaller ones offer more flexibility than large ones when rearranging a floor plan; matched armchairs are more easily paired side-by-side or grouped around a table than mismatched ones. Benches and ottomans are especially adept at playing dual roles – stylish coffee tables for one event, extra seating for the next.

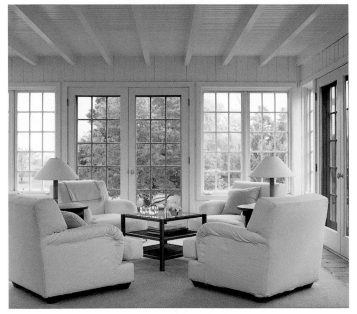

A warm-weather set-up, *above*, puts the sofa in position for admiring the garden view; the grouping's focus is directed away from the fireplace. In autumn and winter, *opposite page*, attention moves to the blazing hearth after a quick rearrangement of sofa and chairs.

A quartet of armchairs, *left*, works as an intimate variation on the classic arrangement of two sofas facing each other. This set-up is ideal for an evening of board games or lively conversation.

DESIGN LESSON ARRANGING SECTIONAL SEATING

Sectional seating is one of the most versatile systems, taking up less space than a combination of chairs and sofas. The absence of arms on many designs also contributes to a sense of openness. Systems are usually sold in units (corners plus one-armed or armless chairs, chaise longues, and sofas), letting you adapt seating to your needs. Armless units offer the most flexibility.

U Arrangement
Offering maximum seating, its scale may call for larger companion pieces like an oversize ottoman in place of a coffee table; allow 45 cm (18 in) clearance.

Corner Arrangement
Sections of equal length should be balanced with a large-scaled chair. Instead of using a coffee table, you might use a sideboard behind one or both sections.

L Arrangement
A rectangular coffee table completes an L-shaped seating group. In a tight space, nesting tables kept at one end are a useful alternative to a coffee table.

Fireplace Options

People are naturally drawn to fire, and a hearth is one of the most inviting focal points in a home. Due to its visual significance, a fireplace is often a room's most important structural element, too. Because a fireplace tends to dominate a room, even small changes to its mantel, surround, or hearth can have a big impact.

If your existing fireplace is less than perfect, all is not lost. Often the surface elements and scale can be improved (see below) without changing the fireback or chimney, which are more complicated projects. Ideally, a fireplace's style and scale should match the room's architecture and should be as accessible and inviting as possible. Consider whether you want a deep mantel or a shallow one, a colourful inner surround of tiles or stone or something more subdued. Luxurious materials like marble and granite add lustre to fireplace surrounds, mantels, and hearths, and using them in such a small area yields a great effect at a relatively modest cost.

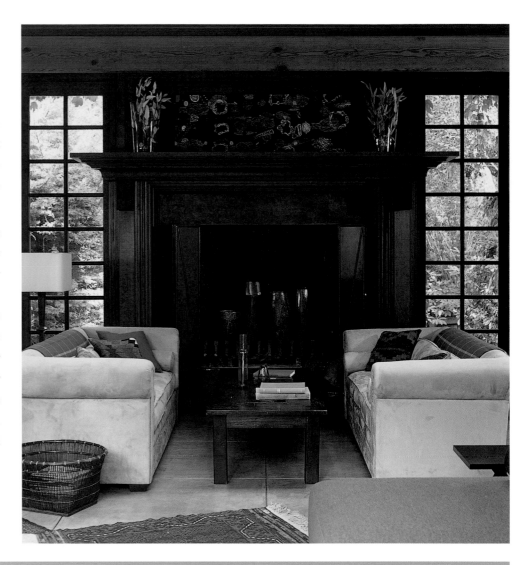

A Rumford fireplace, *right*, is an 18th-century design that features a high opening and a shallow fireback to project radiant heat. A tall, vertical fireback matches the scale of rooms with high ceilings.

DESIGN LESSON GIVE YOUR FIREPLACE A NEW LOOK

mantel

surround of non-combustible material

fireback

hearth

Should you find yourself faced with an oddly proportioned or deteriorated fireplace, look first at simple ways to update its appearance. Several intermediate measures, from painting or resurfacing to installing a new mantel, can improve the look of an old fireplace for a fraction of what a complete replacement might cost. The materials listed at right are available at most DIY and fireplace stores.

Depending upon your home repair skills, it may be wiser to hire a carpenter or tiler to do the work for you rather than try to tackle it yourself. Fireback structural repairs should always be done by a professional.

■ CLEANING SOLUTIONS for hearths and stone remove soot and smoke stains.

■ FRESH PAINT offers the quickest and most affordable way to give dated or unattractive brick fireplaces a new look.

■ NEW MANTELS vary greatly in style, from custom-cut marble or limestone to pre-fabricated wood or stone, cement, "cast-stone", or even iron versions. Most DIY stores and timber yards carry a range of models, including antique reproductions.

■ REPLACEMENT SURROUNDS, whether fashioned from stone slabs cut to size or made of ceramic or stone tiles, can usually be applied directly to existing surfaces, or the surfaces can be replastered with stucco.

Corner Hearth

Where wall space is at a premium, building a fireplace into a corner is an attractive option that lends a cosy mood to any room. Seating groups orientated towards a corner position bring fresh dimension to a room, and benches along one or both sides of a fireplace make it even more inviting.

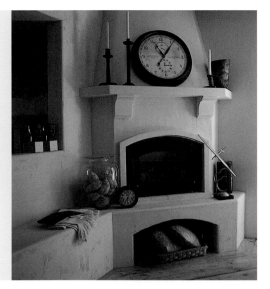

Traditional Wood

Wooden mantels were historically made in the architectural style of the house, and you should aim for the same compatibility. With salvaged mantels and reproductions available in Arts and Crafts, Edwardian, Victorian, Art Deco, and many other styles, it's easy to find a mantel that reflects your home's character.

Flush Mantel

A shallow or flush mantel is an ideal choice for a smaller room. This slender moulding of faux stone adds architectural detail without overpowering the room or occupying too much space. It extends out from the wall just enough to gracefully frame the opening and support a painting on its ledge.

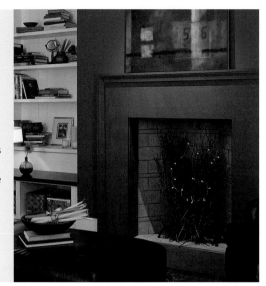

Raised Hearth

A hearth that sits about 45 cm (18 in) above the floor puts the fire at a height where it is more easily seen from anywhere in the room. It also simplifies the task of starting and maintaining a fire. The hearth can be extended to either side to create a low bench for fireside seating.

Antique Stone

This small-scale iron fireplace with marble mantelpiece was originally designed to burn coal but has been converted to burn wood. Its beautifully incised surround, arched fireback, and simple mantel need no further embellishment. Reproductions of antique surrounds and mantels are widely available.

Hole-in-the-Wall

This minimalist approach defines a current trend in fireplace design that's become popular in contemporary homes. Another example of a fireplace style that evolves from architecture, the hole-in-the-wall fireplace generally features a horizontal fireback, positioned low on the wall, with no mantel or surround.

MANTEL DISPLAYS SET A TONE
FOR A LIVING ROOM. ALLOW
YOUR FAVOURITE COLLECTIONS
TO TAKE CENTRE STAGE.

A Federal-style mirror,
top left, is given eclectic
companions in this asym-
metrical composition. The
objects are united by a black,
tan, and white colour scheme.
Choose pieces that repeat
basic forms (the balls echo the
round mirror), then adjust your
arrangement until you've
achieved a pleasing balance.

A cinephile's collection, *left*,
pairs vintage film posters with
a row of antique cameras and
equipment for a witty homage
to cinema history.

A natural theme, *above*, unifies
this display. The repetition of
round and rectangular shapes
gives a sense of rhythm and
movement to the grouping,
drawing the eye from the shells
to the flowers, then up to the
unusually framed book hung
on the wall above.

A group of magnifying glasses,
right, is mixed with black-and-
white pottery pieces for a
whimsical display. The grouping
creates a dynamic line-up of
shapes brought together by
a common colour palette.

The trend of having an open-plan family space has become increasingly common in today's homes. It's easy to see why. Perhaps nothing enhances family life as much as a room that's generous enough for everyone to occupy together, and well designed enough for them to do it harmoniously. The trick to making an open space work is balancing a desire for some degree of separation with a need for overall harmony. Begin by zoning the room for different activities – reading, film

PLANNING A
SHARED SPACE

WITH SO MANY FAMILIES TRADING FORMAL LIVING AND DINING ROOMS FOR AN ALL-PURPOSE "GREAT ROOM", A SHARED OPEN SPACE IS BECOMING THE NEW HEART OF THE HOME.

watching, dining, and so on. This helps establish a sense of having intimate areas within the larger space. Signal transitions from one activity zone to another with rugs and strategic furniture groupings. Unify the space by sticking to a single cohesive style, and use just one or two principal colours throughout to minimize visual clutter. Choose materials, finishes, and fabrics that stand up well to constant use, furniture that's generously scaled, and multiple sources of both ambient and task lighting. Give special attention to display, and allow plenty of space for storage – an especially important element here, where so many activities are at play.

PLANNING A SHARED SPACE

A Well-Mannered Family Room

Music and games are part of the household routine in a refined family room whose comfortable style gets dressed for company.

Sometimes you need a room that's designed for quiet grown-up gatherings and leisure time at the piano, but you also need space for family get-togethers and game playing. An understated decorative scheme is the best solution for a refined and easy-going family space.

Comfort and elegance combine beautifully in a room whose palette is drawn from muted neutrals and earth tones. Neutrals are always the most flexible backdrop, as the look of a room can be freshened quickly with a change of accents. Warm neutrals convey a low-key luxury that's easy to dress up or down: curl up with the kids at play and the dogs at your feet, then host a cocktail party later that evening. Temper a room's formality with decidedly informal furnishings such as leather armchairs and a casual wool-pile rug, and keep accessories simple and graphic.

Zoning Strategies

Give shape to an open-plan room with subtle dividing lines that preserve its openness while creating discrete areas for all of its uses.

The challenge of an open floor plan is finding ways to define zones for different activities – or different family members – while maintaining a luxurious sense of space. Creating visual divisions between zones is usually the best strategy. Facing a sectional sofa away from the rest of an open space can demarcate seating, dining, or work areas. Partial walls, bookcases, folding screens, and portières (curtains used as screens) are also effective room dividers; by stopping short of the ceiling, they preserve a room's openness. Zones can also be delineated by a change in flooring materials or a difference in ceiling heights.

As a general rule, a few large-scale pieces of furniture make a greater impact in an open space than a line-up of smaller pieces, which can create a disorderly look. Sectional pieces or flexible pairs are practical choices because they help to define activity areas and are easily rearranged as your needs change.

WHY THIS ROOM WORKS

Designed for a family with young children, this open space uses imaginative visual divisions to establish distinct zones for relaxing, playing, dining, and cooking.

■ A NEUTRAL PALETTE of white and taupe unifies the room's different areas. Bursts of red and decorative notes of ebony add vitality and contrast.

■ A GENEROUS BUILT-IN SOFA defines a comfortable TV-watching area and visually separates the crafts workspace tucked behind it. Suspended red lampshades emphasize the distinction between living and dining areas.

■ A PARTITION WALL screens a kitchen work zone from view and establishes the bold red accent colour that's used throughout the room.

■ CHILD-FRIENDLY FABRICS and scuff-proof floors make this a space where kids are welcome to play freely. The blackboard coffee table on wheels can be moved to other areas of the room. A unique wheeled dining table is expandable, allowing it to be adjusted or moved to accommodate groups of different sizes.

Family-Friendly Living

When the whole family shares a small space, every inch counts. Closed cupboards and portable containers keep things tidy.

Small spaces need smart planning, and that's especially true when several family members all need a place to pursue their work or creative interests within one room. Keeping everyone's equipment, playthings, books, and art supplies organized and easily accessible requires a variety of tailor-made storage solutions.

Bins on wheels make it easy for kids to cart toys or art supplies to where they're needed. Assigning each child his or her own storage bin helps keep belongings orderly and encourages pride of ownership; it also makes kids more likely to pitch in at tidying-up time. Utilize the space under a coffee table to hold baskets of books and toys where children can reach them. Adults' more expensive "toys", like audio and video equipment, are best housed behind doors that can be firmly shut, so closed cupboards are their perfect home.

WHY THIS ROOM WORKS

This family room keeps storage for kids' belongings within their reach at floor-level, while the parents' workstation and audiovisual equipment remain better protected.

■ FLOOR-TO-CEILING CUPBOARDS conceal a television and other equipment when not in use, and offer off-season storage space above.

■ ROLLING BINS and stackable toy boxes allow for quick clearing up. Baskets of children's books are stowed beneath a sturdy coffee table.

■ AN OLD-STYLE SCHOOL DESK gives kids workspace, where they can do artwork and still be near the family.

■ OPEN SHELVING creates a home-office workstation and gives adults easy access to supplies and equipment.

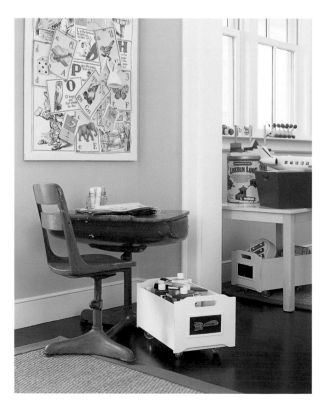

Shelving Options

Bookshelves are among the most efficient of storage options. They also add architectural interest to a room and allow great opportunities for creative expression, displaying not only book collections, but also family mementos, photographs, and artwork.

Shelving should be consistent with a room's overall decorative scheme. Wood is the most common choice because it can be stained or painted to match the existing trim; metal shelves give a more contemporary look. For a clean fit, align edges and tops of shelves with doors, windows, or other architectural elements in the same visual plane. Well-designed bookcases have consistent spacing of vertical supports and, ideally, horizontal shelves are positioned in one continuous line for the length of the unit (though shelf heights may vary to hold diverse objects, electronic equipment, or large books). Plan to have the largest openings at the bottom, to avoid a top-heavy or skewed appearance.

Wraparound bookshelves, *right*, turn a corner of an open-plan room into a reading nook with deep window sills and a handsome display shelf at ceiling height. Extending shelves across the tops of the windows gives the unit a tailored look.

DESIGN LESSON ORGANIZING BOOKS ON SHELVES

Once you have your bookshelves in place, it's time to put them to work. You might not think of filling shelves as a design decision, but a well-planned arrangement that mixes books with favourite objects makes an attractive display that's easy to access. Bookshelf displays are an intimate revelation of the soul of the family. Books and mementos announce areas of particular interest, favourite authors and artists, and memorable family trips. If you'd like to reorganize your shelves, for a more handsome display or simply to make it easier to find particular books, here are some guidelines that will turn your wall of storage into a handsome room decoration as well.

■ TAKE STOCK of what you need to shelve. Remove everything and sort it by size or genre, so you can see what you've got to work with.

■ LEAVE SPACES within the upright books for placing objects or collections, or to hang artwork on the wall or bookcase back. This essentially creates display cases within the shelves, which lightens the overall look of the bookcases.

■ ARRANGE BOOKS BY SIZE: The most visually pleasing arrangements place the larger books and objects on the bottom shelves and smaller items up higher. As you fill shelves, allow 3–5 cm (1–2 in) clearance above each row of books.

■ ADD CONTAINERS to hold loose items and maintain an orderly look. Use baskets or storage boxes for photos, maps, and letters.

Uniform Cubes

Wall-to-wall shelves composed of uniformly sized cubes reduce the span between vertical supports – one way to minimize sagging of the shelves over time. The orderly grid also works well for displays of books and diverse objects.

Free-standing

A trio of 30 cm- (12 in-) deep bookcases transforms a stair landing into a mini-library and still leaves plenty of room for foot traffic. Lined up flush along a wall, free-standing bookcases mimic the look of costlier built-in ones.

Fireplace Framing

The walls on either side of a fireplace are a natural location for shelving. In this configuration, the top shelf extends across the fireplace, unifying the entire wall and forming a frame for displaying artwork above the mantel. Leaving the top shelf empty gives it a more tailored look.

Space Efficient

All you need for bookshelves is a depth of 30 cm (12 in), and that can be found in the most unexpected places around your home. Under-window shelving makes the most of unused space, creating a surface for displays or a base for window seating.

Wraparound

Over-the-door shelving has long been popular with book lovers short on space, and it also adds architectural interest. When shelving uprights frame a door or window, they make it appear to be recessed.

Painted Background

Paint the wall behind your shelving a deep contrasting colour to call attention to decorative objects interspersed among the ranks of books. In floor-to-ceiling bookcases, varying the vertical spacing between shelves within the grid creates a more dynamic arrangement.

LIVING WITH BOOKS IS AN EVERYDAY PLEASURE. CREATIVE DISPLAYS LET YOU SHOW OFF FAVOURITE TITLES THAT REVEAL A BIT ABOUT WHO YOU ARE.

A long shadow box, *above*, turns a stack of books into a witty display. The box is filled with a colourful collection of pulp-fiction paperbacks, and its back is lined with enlargements of pages from the books, a clever personal touch that gives the arrangement a finished look.

Paper-wrapped books, *right*, form a sleek and slightly tongue-in-cheek arrangement, stacked and topped with favourite objects. White paper harmonizes disparate dust jackets, and handwritten titles on the spines give them a casual, personalized appearance.

A row of cookery books, *opposite top*, is kept tidy and made more decorative by a collection of vintage graters, used to separate groups of titles. Equally suited to the task would be cloth bags of rice or flour, vintage food tins with period labels, wooden cutting boards, or other collections of culinary objects.

A bookstore-style arrangement, *opposite bottom*, places a handful of titles face out, a set-up that varies a bookcase's visual grid and invites guests to browse. Change the display to highlight different titles or to feature a recently read favourite.

There was a time when a proper living room was arranged like a stage set and decorated to demonstrate a family's standing in the world. Reserved for special occasions, a living room required formal behaviour. The new living room, though, is all about comfort, and goes a step beyond welcoming family and friends in style. It should be a place where you feel equally at home taking an afternoon nap or hosting a cocktail party, and a place where your children want to bring friends home

PROVIDING
COMFORT

WHEN A GUEST SLIPS OFF HER SHOES AND CURLS UP ON YOUR SOFA LIKE A CONTENTED CAT, TAKE IT AS A COMPLIMENT. YOU'VE SERVED UP THE GREATEST LUXURY: TRUE COMFORT.

to play. Comfort means putting people at ease, both physically and emotionally. The ingredients are simple: commodious furnishings, soft textures, and thoughtful touches that invite guests to relax. It's about flattering light, a plump cushion for a friend to press into the crook of his back or rest behind his neck, and extra chairs for last-minute guests. It's the touch of soft leather, the spring of a pile rug, the scent of fresh flowers. Add the flicker of candlelight, an embroidered cushion, and a soft throw to toss over bare feet, and you're there. True comfort comes from being surrounded by loved ones and enjoying the beauty of home.

Warm jewel tones, candlelight, and sensuous materials add luxurious accents to an informal living room that anyone can feel at home in.

■ CASUAL LOOSE COVERS, paired with cushions and throws in sumptuous fabrics, strike a perfect balance between laid-back and elegant.

■ ANTIQUE AND NEW PIECES are mixed for a relaxed mood.

■ WARM CHOCOLATE WALLS create a cocoon-like feeling. Earth tones, even in deep shades, can work as neutrals in a sophisticated palette like this one.

■ BAMBOO BLINDS are a more informal choice than curtains.

■ A WOOL RUG introduces pattern to the room, adding depth to the decor.

PROVIDING COMFORT

A Textural Blend

A soothing haven for family and friends layers on comfort in the form of deeply textured fabrics, warm colours, and luxurious accents.

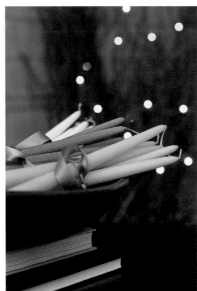

Your home can look elegant and sophisticated and still be inviting and comfortable. The secret lies in giving rooms an appealing textural mix – combining furnishings and accents to create spaces that are stylish but that still put everyone at ease.

Keep the mood easy and uncomplicated by layering basic furniture pieces with fabrics that reward the senses, such as a plush shawl or throw tossed over the back of a sofa. Rich wall colours, leather, wood, and soft lamplight all contribute depth and warmth to a space. At nightfall, candlelight casts a warm glow.

A combination of casual and luxurious fabrics keeps a room looking polished but feeling comfortable. Dress up cotton loose covers with cushions and throws of supple leather, suede, or velvet. Cotton velvet, damask, and chenille are all lush-looking fabrics that have the added benefit of easy care. Quilted, tufted, or ruched fabrics also heighten a room's sense of luxury.

A Restful Palette

To create a room as restorative as an old-time summer hotel, keep the colours and furnishings simple and maximize natural light.

Comfort comes in many forms, but few things are as soothing as daylight playing across a palette of serene colours. Rooms with a subdued colour scheme have a calming effect, especially when furnishings are soft and understated and accent hues are reserved.

In an all-white room, variations in texture are essential for variety. Wood panelling, rustic antiques, natural woven rugs, wicker furniture, quilted linen, and flowers and other natural objects all add textural interest. If privacy is not an issue, leave windows bare to let in daylight, and enjoy the interplay with nature. Outdoor furniture, such as rattan or wicker pieces, can be fitted with comfortable cushions, lending natural style to a room.

WHY THIS ROOM WORKS

The natural light streaming into this room gives it a rare serenity and freshness, with just enough contrast to engage the eye and plenty of cool green to soothe it.

■ GENEROUS SEATING makes this a welcoming space, whether you're hosting a whole crowd or looking for a spot to snooze.

■ AN ALL-WHITE COLOUR PALETTE, accented with a range of greens, changes with the shifting light throughout the day.

■ NATURAL TEXTURES, from the wicker chairs and sisal rug to the worn woods and soft fabrics, add interest to the monochromatic colour scheme.

■ ABUNDANT GREENERY in flower arrangements and potted topiaries brings the outdoors in.

■ IMPROMPTU ACCENTS reinforce a casual air. A whimsically framed botanical print on the mantel is surrounded by garden clippings.

Once you've created an inviting living area inside your home, extend what you love about the room outdoors to your garden or patio. Increasingly, home-loving nesters view the near outdoors not as a separate realm but as a natural extension of the home. In keeping with a desire for a more casual lifestyle, relaxing and entertaining out-of-doors have become more prevalent because they requires less fuss and planning than they do indoors, plus it's easier to include children in the

EXTENDING OUTDOORS

OUR HOMES ARE OPENING UP TO EMBRACE THE OUTDOORS AS NEVER BEFORE. THE CHERISHED OLD VERANDA, PATIO, AND TERRACE HAVE BECOME THE NEW LIVING ROOM.

festivities. And with all the water-resistant furnishings and fabrics now widely available, you can decorate your deck or patio with the same sense of style and forethought that you use indoors. Hallways, too, are enjoying new attention. What once was just a way in and out of the house is now being treated with the same respect and care as other rooms. Once you get outdoors, it's now easier to stay there longer – especially in regions where the climate is temperate for much of the year. Thanks to patio heaters, canopied terraces, fire pits, and outdoor fireplaces, everyone can enjoy the garden, deck, patio, or veranda as their year-round retreat.

Surrounded by lush plantings and flooded with air and light, this gracious patio offers all the best of indoor–outdoor living.

■ A DEEP PERGOLA with climbing bougainvillea vines affords filtered shade by day and provides a sense of enclosure.

■ WEATHERPROOF CHAIRS fitted with water-resistant fabric cushions are the outdoor equivalent of indoor easy chairs.

■ MULTIPLE FRENCH WINDOWS run the length of the patio, blurring the line between indoors and out and providing easy access to interior rooms and food and supplies.

■ A FREE-STANDING BAR can be brought indoors and used off-season.

EXTENDING OUTDOORS

An Easy Transition

The best outdoor spaces blur the boundaries between house and garden and marry beautiful surroundings with indoor amenities.

One of the many pleasures of an outdoor room is the sense of being partly in nature, partly sheltered from it. To heighten this feeling, make the transition from indoors to out as seamless as possible. Arrange furniture groupings as you would indoors, and define the edges of the exterior space with a change of paving or a shift from paving to lawn or gravel. Clear views and easy access between inside and out – large French windows are ideal – are key in creating a sense of flow.

Choose furniture made of teak or other moisture-resistant woods that can be left outside to slowly weather to a silver-grey. Use plump cushions and fabrics that are both water- and mould-resistant for lasting wear. Any lighting that you add should be subtle; supplement it with soft candlelight, using windproof hurricane lamps or oversize lanterns. Setting up an outdoor bar or serving table cuts down on trips to the kitchen, letting you spend more time with guests.

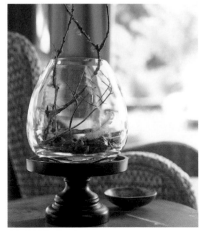

EXTENDING OUTDOORS

Inside-Out Living

A stone fireplace transforms a breezy summer veranda into a year-round gathering place for open-air relaxation and enjoyment.

A sheltered veranda has always been more than just a pleasant place to pass the time. Verandas are like treehouses for adults, with a special aura that softens the poignancy of summer's end. A trend towards including outdoor fireplaces on verandas, decks, and patios, however, now makes it possible to extend the outdoor living season long past summer's end. Just as in a traditional living room, a fireplace provides a natural focal point around which to build an outdoor room.

Especially if you enjoy a seasonally dry climate, you have more options in outdoor furnishings. Furniture made of rustproof metals or moisture-resistant hard-woods such as teak, redwood, and nyatoh can be supplemented with lightweight, portable furnishings and accent pieces from indoors. Rugs, colourful throws, extra cushions, and even reading lamps make it more enjoyable to settle in. For a greater sense of enclosure, hang curtains made from all-weather fabric.

Inviting Hallways

Hallways offer a first impression of your home, so it's especially important to consider their dual nature when decorating them. As a practical matter, hallways are about comings and goings, so you need a smart system for managing clutter in one of the home's smallest rooms. On an emotional level, halls are about being welcomed and celebrated, so you'll want to include touches that make each arrival feel like an event.

Making it all work begins with storage that brings order to the space. If your hallway has no cupboard, hang hooks on the walls for coats and hats, and provide bins or baskets for wet boots and umbrellas. Designate a place to set packages, post, and keys, such as on a hall table or sideboard. A chair or bench to sit on and remove shoes is also a thoughtful addition. To visually link the hall to the rest of the house, use furnishings, colours, and decorative accents that are similar to the adjoining rooms. And don't forget to lay out a welcome mat!

A sturdy sideboard, *right*, provides a hardworking storage system for a busy household hallway. Extra containers for larger items leave a clear path for coming-and-going traffic, and wall hooks turn a row of hats into a decorative yet practical display.

DESIGN LESSON CHOOSING FLOORING FOR HALLWAYS

Whether your door opens into a foyer or directly onto the main living space, a hallway's flooring takes a lot of wear. It also has to make a positive first impression. The kind of flooring you choose helps to establish not only the tone of the hallway but also of the rest of your house.

Dual concerns influence the choice of materials here: formality and wearability. An elegant style of decor or a formal house exterior might call for a dignified introduction. Similarly, casual interiors should be announced by an informal hallway. You can make a foyer seem bigger than it actually is by using the same flooring in it as the rooms it adjoins. This may mean sacrificing durability in the hall for appearance in the adjoining rooms, if you choose wood instead of tile, for instance.

■ WOOD, *top left*, is warm, beautiful, and smooth underfoot but requires periodic refinishing and protection in wet weather.

■ PORCELAIN TILE, *top right*, is made from a special mix of clays and minerals that can be fired at an extremely high temperature, yielding a hard, dense tile that resists stains and scratches. Large-format porcelain tiles are often designed to look like stone.

■ TEXTURED STONE, *bottom left*, is a versatile option that complements a wide range of styles. It adds instant luxury and stands up well to everyday use.

■ TERRACOTTA TILE, *bottom right*, offers a warm, rustic look. Because it's unglazed, it requires sealing but is otherwise easy-care.

Painted Wooden Gate

A front gate should be inviting while reflecting the style of the house behind it. This cheerful carved wooden gate echoes the rustic style of the rammed-earth house just beyond. Open panels are a friendly touch, making the gate less imposing, and its bright colour keeps it festive.

Grille Gate

Transparency makes a sturdy gate seem less imposing and more welcoming. This beautiful scrolled wrought-iron gate, which invites visitors to peek down the garden walk, is a recycled vintage window, as strong as it is beautiful. Its dramatic style heightens the pleasure of arrival.

Staircase Entrance

Make the most of an older house's stair-dominated entrance by highlighting architectural details with glossy paint and laying down a stair runner, to add interest and lead the eye upward. This "runner" is cleverly painted onto the stairs, leading the eye to a stack of vintage suitcases, which double as off-season storage.

Living Room Entrance

When a front door opens directly into a living room, define an "entrance" with a large piece of furniture such as a sideboard or cupboard. Hooks placed high on the wall turn coats and other belongings into an artful display. A drawer conceals the keys, gloves, scarves, and post that often accumulate.

Mudroom

Cowboy bunkhouse style suits a weekend retreat or might be used in the garage or utility entrance of a busy household. Personalized "cubicles" are labelled with blackboards, making it easy for everyone to find their hats, boots, and rain gear on the way out — and to put them back in place on the way in.

Half-Wall

Open rooms need a transitional space, too. Where no defined entrance to a room exists, create a sense of a foyer with a free-standing unit like this high-backed bench. It gives people a place to sit and take off boots or muddy shoes, has a handy storage compartment within its bench, and hides an area behind it that's used for storing outdoor gear.

The display of things that are personally meaningful is among the most democratic of art forms, and one of the most engaging. What is comforting to family is often fascinating to guests, and what we respond to most in a room is personal expression. Put on view the artwork, photos, and objects that you love – creatively using shelving, mantels, table surfaces, and wall spaces – and let them tell a story about your interests, heritage, and travels. Special pieces and collections are among the

SHOWCASING
FAVOURITE THINGS

DISPLAYS OF TREASURED ITEMS AND PERSONAL COLLECTIONS BRING LIFE TO A HOME. OFFER GUESTS A GLIMPSE INTO YOUR PASSIONS WITH ARTISTIC ARRANGEMENTS IN EVERY ROOM.

most important elements of your home, and though there's no rule about what to include, a few guidelines will help you show your personal favourites to best advantage. Arrange objects and photos for maximum impact, grouped by colour, material, shape, or theme; arrangements in groups of three or five are especially pleasing to the eye. Framed photos of your ancestors, the family farm, and your parents as newlyweds posing in front of their first car take on the poetic sweep of a genealogical chart when seen marching up a stairwell wall. Even antique postcards become a unique gallery when mounted, framed, and proudly displayed.

Shelves for Display

Wall-to-wall shelves are a dramatic showcase for books, singular objects, and collections. Plan ahead for the most effective display.

Few decorating tricks are as transformative as installing a wall of shelves to put books, decorative objects, and art on view. Whether free-standing or built-in, shelving is ideal for displays because it contains clutter, is space-efficient, and can be changed and updated easily.

Vary the height of individual niches to accommodate different-sized items, and mix groups of books, favourite accessories, and found objects in creative ways to add interest. (If favourite things also happen to make clever bookends, all the better.) Painting shelves a uniform colour ensures a clean appearance; a contrasting colour on the back wall makes objects stand out. Accent lighting adds drama; if possible, plan ahead for electrical sockets.

WHY THIS ROOM WORKS

Built-in shelves devoted to art and family treasures animate this room, give it a warm character, and establish order.

■ STRONG HORIZONTALS at table height and at the top of the shelving establish a bold framework for the shelving's grid and highlight the upper tier, which houses a single collection.

■ A QUIET PALETTE allows treasures to stand out against the light grey background; objects on the shelves seem to come forwards visually.

■ LARGER LOWER SHELVES for oversize books are practical and important for visual balance.

■ A PAIR OF LARGER OPENINGS within the grid lend symmetry and create space for displays of artwork.

■ ANTIQUES AND FOUND OBJECTS interspersed among the books provide variety and interest.

■ CONTAINERS for loose change and post make use of whimsical objects.

GROUPING YOUR COLLECTIONS IS A SURE WAY TO CREATE DISPLAYS WITH DRAMA. USE REPETITION OF FORM, COLOUR, AND THEME AS POWERFUL UNIFIERS.

Antique teacups, *above*, and other small, fragile collectables tend to get lost in a large cupboard. These wall-mounted display cubes show off each item to advantage and create a bold pattern against a dark blue wall.

A collection of natural objects, *right*, have greater visual interest when one is given prominence. Here, a delicate ostrich egg is highlighted on a display stand, providing a focal point for the grouping.

An assortment of keys, *opposite top*, reads as a collection when displayed with purpose. The backdrop here is a magnetic bulletin board fitted with rectangular magnets, from which the keys dangle on simple ribbons.

A row of antique weights, *opposite bottom*, gains presence when arranged on a slightly raised tray. This beautiful composition is capped by a colourful accent – a single sprig of bittersweet.

A Home Gallery

Make a bold statement with a wall devoted to a gallery-style display of photographs, ready to change at a moment's notice.

Well–displayed photos can transform a room, whether they're signed works you've collected or prints from your most recent outing with the digital camera. Not only are photographs one of the more affordable forms of art, they also lend themselves to a variety of display styles. If you're working with your own photographs, the options for display are greater still, since you can control the size and cropping of the prints as well.

Instead of hanging framed photos on a wall with nails or tacks, try propping them on narrow shelves. Using shelves makes it easy to rearrange or add new pieces to your gallery. Arrange photos asymmetrically to give the display a sense of dynamism and possibility.

WHY THIS ROOM WORKS

Careful pacing of colour and a sense of restrained luxury make this space surprisingly warm. White walls and furnishings keep the focus on the photo collection.

■ NARROW-LEDGE SHELVES visually recede into the white background but offer plenty of space for an ever-changing gallery. A ceiling-mounted display light illuminates the collection at night.

■ UNFRAMED PHOTOS hang from wire with clips, allowing for quick changes to vary the display's visual pacing.

■ SIMPLE FRAMES in similar styles and colours give the disparate photographs a sense of unity.

■ LOW-PROFILE FURNISHINGS let the colourful photo display take prominence in the space.

■ CAREFULLY CHOSEN ACCESSORIES pick up the strong colours in the photographs and extend them into the room.

HANGING PHOTOGRAPHS IS AN ART UNTO ITSELF. FRAME, MOUNT, AND GROUP IMAGES FOR GREATEST IMPACT, AND FIND UNEXPECTED PLACES TO HANG THEM.

Photos in various sizes, *opposite top*, are arranged asymmetrically and mixed with mirrors and collected objects to form an attractive composition. Harmony is maintained by using only black-and-white images and a consistent colour for all frames. Weaving mementos into your photo display is a compelling way to tell a story.

Black-and-white photos, *opposite bottom*, have a surprising freshness when mounted in a series on the doors of a glossy black cupboard. The collection is uniformly framed in red with identical white mounts. Look beyond your four walls to find interesting places to display photographs: perhaps lined up on the floor leaning against a wall, or resting on ascending shelves mounted along a stairway.

Precisely aligned botanical photos, *left*, bring gallery-style polish to this display. When grouping photographs in a grid, it's usually best to stick to a single subject or theme and to choose either all black-and-white images or all colour. Frames in a grid arrangement often look best when they're identical, though mount size may vary to fit the individual photos. Measure carefully to ensure that you have the same amount of space between frames for a uniform grid.

Panoramic photographs, *above*, are high-lighted by unique placement — beneath a window ledge — intensifying their impact and telling a compelling story in black and white. Arranged in a horizontal row, the pictures allow a narrative to unfold, much like flipping through the pages of a book.

DINING

"I LOVE SHARING FOOD WITH FAMILY AND FRIENDS. I WANT EVERYONE TO FEEL AT HOME IN MY DINING ROOM, FREE TO TALK AND LAUGH FOR HOURS AROUND MY TABLE."

DINING SPACE

Of all the rooms in the house, the dining room is the one that has seen the fewest changes in our lifetimes – at least in terms of basic furnishings and set-up. What has changed is our style of dining. Where formal rooms and fancy place settings were once the norm, we now enjoy relaxed elegance in open-plan spaces, take meals at the kitchen island or in an open courtyard, and use a dining area as a home base that welcomes activity outside mealtimes. Our dining spaces are also warmer and more personal than ever before.

The rooms on the following pages illustrate just a few of the options available for creating livable dining spaces indoors and out, and making them a highlight of your home.

How to Plan a Dining Space

The dining room is by nature a simple space, but it can lend itself to spirited styling. After all, its main function is celebration. Look for quality and comfort in a dining set, then add furnishings that suit your entertaining style.

The centrepiece of any dining space is its table. Wood remains the most common choice, and is popular for its warm patina and easy care. Rich wood finishes suit almost any decorating style, while painted tables tend to be more informal. The surprise of black painted wood freshens a dining space and, like the classic little black dress, it can be informal or sophisticated as the occasion warrants. The style of dining chairs is another key element in creating a distinctive personality for the room. They should gracefully complement the table,

though they need not match it (see pages 98–99 for helpful advice on selecting dining chairs). It's an advantage to have storage for dinnerware located right in your dining room, whether built-in or free-standing. A sideboard is an efficient option that does double duty as a storage piece and serving table. A taller glass-door cupboard or dresser is attractive because it adds height in a room where the furniture tends to be low.

This is a room of primarily hard surfaces, so bring in fabrics to soften and warm the space. Drape the table in crisp linens or casual runners that let the beauty of the wood show through. Hang curtains or fabric blinds at the windows. Drapery panels of velvet or silk catch candlelight beautifully, adding texture, warmth, and a sense of luxury. Upholstered chairs or loose covers offer other ways to introduce colour, pattern, and texture.

CASUAL DINING ROOM

Comfortably furnished with an oval table and armchairs, this room (above and preceding page) invites everyone to settle in for an enjoyable meal.

■ ROUND AND OVAL TABLES are becoming increasingly popular because they naturally stimulate conversation, allowing each person to see and hear all other diners.

■ UPHOLSTERED ARMCHAIRS encourage guests to linger after meals.

■ A WINE CUPBOARD adds character to a dining space. It's also an efficient storage component, with a surface that can be used for buffet service and an upper cupboard that holds glassware and dinnerware as well as displays of collections and objects.

■ A HANDSOME CHANDELIER suggests a festive occasion without the formality of an ornate crystal fixture.

SUN VERANDA

A sideboard provides useful storage of dinnerware and linens.

LIVING ROOM

Pairs of wall sconces on both walls contribute ambient light. Dimmers allow maximum control.

A small table makes coffee and dessert service easy.

CLASSIC DINING ROOM

Several doorways open onto this traditional floor plan, but a 1.2 m (4 ft) passageway prevents congestion. The dining table sits 90 cm (3 ft) away from furniture along the walls to allow space for guests to slide their chairs back.

Two extra chairs flank a small side table; when leaves are added to the dining table, these are easily pulled to the main dining area.

Curtains in the bay window bring soft texture and warmth to the space.

PATIO

KITCHEN

ENTRANCE

OPEN-PLAN DINING AREA

This dining area sits between the living area and the kitchen (at bottom right, not shown). Sliding glass doors on one wall lead to an outdoor patio, so traffic through the room was a main consideration in furniture arrangement.

A sideboard topped by lamps separates the dining space from the living area. It offers convenient storage for dinnerware and a surface for serving buffet dinners, snacks, and drinks.

A large rug helps define the dining area within the open plan. It is 90 cm (36 in) larger than the table on all sides, so it allows chairs to be pulled in and out at the table while still remaining on the rug.

The dining table seats ten people with extra leaves inserted.

HOW MANY PEOPLE CAN YOUR TABLE SEAT?

To prevent diners from bumping elbows with each other, allow at least 60 cm (24 in) of table space for each person.

60 cm (24 in)

Rectangular Table
180 x 81–90 cm (72 x 32–36 in) seats 6
229 x 81–90 cm (90 x 32–36 in) seats 8
274 x 81–90 cm (108 x 32–36 in) seats 10
305 x 81–90 cm (120 x 32–36 in) seats 12

See page 99 to determine how large a table your dining area can accommodate.

Round or Oval Table
A pedestal base offers more flexible seating, allowing you to fit more people.

Round 114 cm (45 in) diameter seats 4
Oval 168 x 114 cm (66 x 45 in) seats 6
Oval 185 x 114 cm (73 x 45 in) seats 6–8

The formal dining room that many of us grew up with is like a three-piece suit: handsome, traditional, and fairly formal. Today's dining rooms are more like an outfit you'd wear on holiday. Comfort is key, and beauty comes from a stylish combination of informal elements. While the classic furniture pieces remain, they are now more comfortable, functional, and in keeping with the style of the rest of your home. You don't even need to have a separate formal room. Carve a dining area out of

REDEFINING THE
DINING ROOM

TODAY'S DINING SPACES ARE RELAXED AND CASUAL, WITH FORMAL TOUCHES COMING FROM WELL-CHOSEN ACCESSORIES AND PLACE SETTINGS RATHER THAN FROM THE ROOM ITSELF.

open space, set up in an extra room, or embrace an open-plan kitchen/dining layout. Furnish your room with unconventional pieces, mismatched chairs, and favourite objects. Store dishware, cutlery, and linen on open shelves in eye-catching vignettes. For a swept-clean look, hang cupboards with glass panes on the wall, or stow tableware in a generous cupboard. Extend a warm welcome by using casual table dressings like place mats, or runners instead of formal linen, and use colourful loose covers and cushions on the chairs. Hang family photos or artwork on the walls, and find every opportunity to give the space your personal stamp.

The New Formal Dining Room

If you love to entertain but your dining room is too small, take advantage of an underused reception room to create a spacious dining area.

Some older homes have an extra reception room that sees little use because residents gravitate towards a larger room or family room. If you have such a space and your formal dining room can't accommodate as many guests as you'd like, why not move your dining table into the extra room? Not only are these rooms frequently larger, they also often have architectural details that make dining more luxurious. Fireplaces add instant warmth, and mantels offer a convenient surface for setting out candles and floral displays. Built-in bookshelves let you showcase personal collections or decorative dishware, making the room feel welcoming.

WHY THIS ROOM WORKS

This former reception room is now a dining area with luxurious seating, ample space, and classic appeal. A simple change of accents dresses the room up or down for fireside suppers or formal dinner parties.

■ A MAHOGANY SIDEBOARD is fitted for wine storage and offers a large surface for wine and cheese service. Decanted bottles of wine hold cheese menus, indicating types that are well suited to the particular vintages.

■ LINEN TABLE RUNNERS suggest a special occasion without the formality of a full tablecloth. They also expose the beauty of the bare wood.

■ LEATHER ARMCHAIRS contrast with linen loose-covered chairs and convey a warm, clublike atmosphere.

■ A LUSH CENTREPIECE adds a sense of abundance that belies its simplicity. It's made from a simple mass of tulips.

■ MANTEL AND SHELVES display art, family photos, and collected objects, personalizing the dining space.

Open-Plan Dining

Wide-open living offers limitless opportunities for creative entertaining. Carve out a dining area, then add warm, welcoming accents.

If you live in an open-plan space, you have the unique opportunity to create "rooms" in your home right where you want them. Without four walls to form a dining room, you can designate one instead with a well-planned arrangement of furnishings.

Laying down a rug is the simplest way to define a dining area within which to arrange your table and chairs. Make sure the rug size is generous enough so that chairs can be pushed back without slipping off. Furniture for storing dinnerware and linen can also be enlisted to further anchor the space. For example, a bar or sideboard might be used to form another "wall" between the dining and living areas.

WHY THIS ROOM WORKS

Dressed in rich colours and warm textures, this dining area in the corner of an open loft has all the comfort and graciousness of a more traditional dining room.

■ A SIDEBOARD BAR at one end of the room helps to define the space. The mirrored wall is a pleasant contrast to the brick and maintains the area's openness.

■ A MIX OF TEXTURES provides visual and tactile interest and makes this a sumptuous place to dine: a paisley throw used as a tablecloth, natural linen loose covers with pleated hems, a patterned rug, and gleaming tableware.

■ BUILT-IN SHELVES installed behind openings in the brick wall serve as an open "butler's pantry" and form an artful display wall.

■ TABLEWARE is attractively stored in and easily accessed from the neat storage and display area. Bundled place settings of cutlery make short work of laying the table.

This contemporary dining room still has the traditional table, chairs, and sideboard but also reflects the owner's strong eye for unique design.

- **AN OPEN SIDEBOARD** offers an opportunity to show off a collection of vintage silver and keeps pieces within reach for use when entertaining.

- **GALLERY-STYLE FRAMED PHOTOS** give the walls character and visual interest without cluttering the space.

- **A NATURAL THEME** pulls the room together. Fig branches serve as a centrepiece, and aspen leaves are a repeated motif on the linen napkins. An abaca rug keeps the mood casual.

- **A GRAPHIC TABLE COVERING** is a photocopy-shop enlargement of a leaf image, protected by Perspex.

REDEFINING THE DINING ROOM

A Fresh Take on Classic Style

It's time to update the definition of "classic". Give a time-honoured set-up a new twist by taking a contemporary approach to design.

The traditional recipe for dining room furnishing calls for a table for six or eight plus a sideboard. This recipe doesn't specify what the pieces must look like, however, or how they ought to be dressed. Reinterpret the formula using your own fresh approach, and bring up-to-the-moment appeal to the classic set-up.

Some people save their favourite things to display in other parts of the house, but decorative items are more than welcome in a dining room, where they can be appreciated throughout the course of a meal. Display collections of silver or servingware, and use the walls as a gallery to hang rows of photographs or artwork. Keep the table simple, with modest settings and a striking centrepiece. Mix delicate antique pieces with strong contemporary styles – hotel silver with simple white dinnerware, for example.

Lighting Options

The basics of lighting in the dining room are simple: indirect light is always better than direct; illumination from lamps and candles should flatter guests; and flexibility is key. Design a versatile lighting plan so that light can be adjusted for time of day or occasion.

A mix of indirect ambient and direct task lighting is best for the table, where you often may be doing more than just dining. Chandeliers are most common for dining room ambient lighting. Pendant fixtures, recessed downlights, or wall-mounted gallery lights can provide a blend of both ambient and task light. Dimmer switches offer extra control and flexibility. Accent lighting adds drama: use picture lights or spotlights to highlight art, objects, or architectural features, and make generous use of candlelight for atmosphere.

Whatever the mix of lighting, the styles you choose convey tone. For example, votive candles create a casual mood, while tapers suggest a more formal occasion.

A properly hung chandelier, *right*, casts light onto the table without shining into diners' eyes. It should be scaled to the size of the table and should never obstruct views across it.

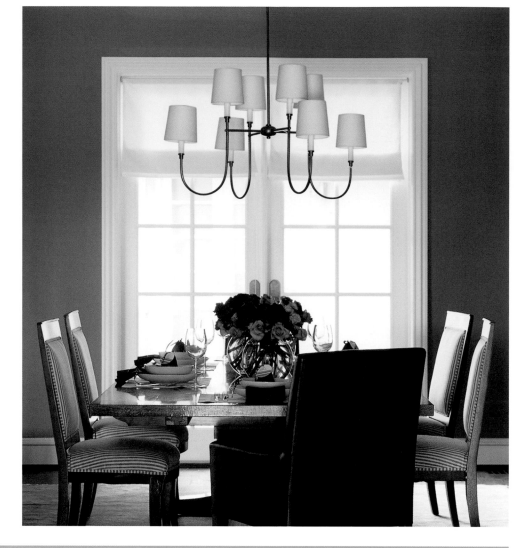

DESIGN LESSON PLANNING FOR CHANDELIERS

What size chandelier will work best with your table? Measure the diameter of a round table or the width of a rectangular table and subtract 30 cm (12 in) to determine the chandelier size that best complements the table. For example, if you have a 105 cm- (42 in-) wide table, your chandelier should be 75 cm (30 in) in diameter. This simple formula assures choosing a fixture that will neither overpower the table nor appear too small for it. A properly proportioned chandelier comes to within 15 cm (6 in) of each edge of the table.

How to hang a chandelier
If you have 2.4 m (8 ft) ceilings, the bottom of the chandelier should be 76 cm (30 in) above the table top. If your ceilings are higher than 2.4 m, raise the chandelier 8 cm (3 in) for every extra 30 cm (1 ft) of height. The chandelier should be centred on the table, even if the electrical connection in the ceiling is not. Use a length of decorative chain to carry the wiring to the chandelier, which should be hung from a secure hook over the centre of the table.

240 cm (8 ft)

76 cm (2.5 ft)

Pendant Lights, *right*
Hanging pendants shed ample direct light over this kitchen work surface and breakfast bar. Because opaque shades don't throw light over a large area, multiple lights are necessary to cover an expansive space.

Table Lamps, *far right*
Balanced light is essential in a dining room, to illuminate its perimeter as well as the table. Wall sconces traditionally provide lighting for a sideboard but can be difficult or expensive to install. Table lamps, set on side tables and wired with dimmers, are an attractive and versatile alternative.

Pillar Candles, *right*
This ring chandelier holds pillar candles in varying sizes and offers an unusual, informal overhead lighting option. Similar chandeliers are available in electric versions that mimic the look of candlelight.

Chandelier, *far right*
A chandelier can be fanciful or tailored; the choice depends more on your style than on a generalized prescription. Once reserved only for grand dining rooms, chandeliers are now often used in family dining areas, too. Often, a room will require supplemental lighting; use recessed downlights, sconces, or table lamps.

Wooden Chairs

All-purpose wooden chairs are available in a wide range of styles. The type of wood and finish influences the formality of the room, with painted wooden chairs being perhaps the most informal. Seat cushions provide additional comfort and bring style to the decor through colour and pattern.

Armchairs

These comfortable chairs encourage lingering at the table, inviting you to sit back, rest your arms, and settle in for coffee and dessert. Armchairs are often used at either end of the table for the hosts but can be used for all seating. The key to using armchairs is making sure that the arms clear the bottom edge of the table.

Loose-covered

Fabric loose covers provide another opportunity to introduce pattern and colour into a room of hard surfaces. Loose covers also give a dining space great flexibility. They can be swapped out seasonally, changed to suit a formal or informal occasion, and are easily removed for cleaning.

Upholstered

Chairs covered in fabric or supple leather are a traditional choice for comfort and afford a polished appearance. They work with almost any decorating scheme, whether formal or casual. Many chairs are covered in easy-care fabrics, and leathers are made more durable and stain-resistant now, so it's easy to maintain their finish.

Stacking Chairs

Lightweight portable chairs are among the most convenient styles to use. They transition effortlessly between casual gatherings and sit-down dinners, and are easy to store in multiples or move around a room. Stacking chairs add a contemporary accent to a traditional dining space.

Traditional Styles

Classic styles like Windsor (shown here), ladderback, and Hitchcock bring a traditional note to a dining space. The curvaceous lines of Windsor chairs visually soften the geometry of a rectangular table; the simple design of a ladderback chair adds height to a sleek dining table; and the petite scale of Hitchcock chairs make them a versatile choice.

Seating Options

The best dining rooms are as comfortable as they are visually appealing. To arrive at the best and most relaxed seating arrangement, begin with a spacious table that works well for a variety of tasks, including dining and working, then look for chairs scaled to the size of your dining space. To ensure comfortable seating and adequate elbow room around the table, allow at least 60 cm (24 in) of space for each person.

While a matched table and chairs give a cohesive look, mixing contemporary with antique styles – or pairing a wooden table with loose-covered, wicker, painted, or leather chairs – affords you the opportunity to show some personal flair. The options for mixing and matching are unlimited, but make sure there is room to slide chairs in and out from the table easily, and note that the position of a table's legs affects how many chairs will fit comfortably. A pedestal-base table allows for more flexible seating than a table with legs.

Long, cushioned benches, *left*, are an unexpected stand-in for traditional dining room chairs. White-painted wooden chairs at either end of the pleasingly scuffed table round out the seating plan, giving this room a relaxed, informal feeling.

DESIGN LESSON WHAT SIZE DINING TABLE?

How large a dining table will your room accommodate? It's easy to calculate the best size for your space. Just base it upon the room's dimensions.

Measuring for a Dining Table
Draw a floor plan to indicate the length and width of the room and any doors and windows that affect furniture placement. Designate a spot for a sideboard or other cupboard, usually 60 cm (24 in) deep. Determine how people will pass through the room and, working from the walls inwards, block out 1.2 m (4 ft) for traffic. Allow at least 90 cm (3 ft) of space from all walls and furniture to pull chairs in and out easily. The space that remains in the centre tells you how much room you have for a table.

4 m (13 ft)

90 cm (3 ft) away from wall or furniture

1.8 m (6 ft)

90 cm (3 ft)

4.5 m (15 ft)

2.1 m (7 ft)

1.2 m (4 ft) for passage

90 cm (3 ft)

The secret to enjoying entertaining – and to doing it successfully – is learning to make it easy on yourself. When you've developed a system for making parties go smoothly, it allows for more spontaneity than if you have to reinvent things each time. It also makes it more likely that you'll want to entertain more frequently. The most important thing to remember is that your aim is to make guests feel celebrated, and that doesn't require much time or work. Focus on the details that create a

ENTERTAINING
WITH STYLE

CLOSE FRIENDS, DELICIOUS FOOD, AND BEAUTIFUL SURROUNDINGS ARE ESSENTIAL TO A CELEBRATION, BUT THOUGHTFUL DETAILS AND CREATIVE TOUCHES GIVE A PARTY ITS STYLE.

memorable party. This is the time to bring out the hotel silver and linen tablecloths, or to dress the table with bright fabrics and colourful flowers. Make the room glow with decorative candles or lanterns, and stemware that adds reflective dazzle. Simple touches like handwritten menu cards or festive party favours placed at each setting signal the beginning of a memorable occasion. Cleverly personalized settings bring touches of whimsy to the table – place cards fashioned from photos, luggage tags, or mini chalkboards, and napkin rings made from beads, buttons, or strands of grasses. Your inventive creations are the touches that add distinctive style to your parties.

Dramatic Practicality

The best entertaining spaces deftly combine drama with good planning and make it easy to host elegant dinners and festive parties.

If you have a lot of things you need to store, sometimes the best solution is to put them all on display. Storage as display is not a new idea, but it can work especially well in a dining space, where many pieces are so shapely and appealing that they create naturally dramatic displays. For day-to-day use, some people also keep a table laid at all times, to encourage the family to sit down together instead of eating in front of the TV.

A wall of floor-to-ceiling shelves filled with tableware, stemware, and cutlery makes a striking decorative statement. It's also highly practical, since items are kept within reach during parties. Set up a bar in an area out of the flow of traffic, and outfit it with an ample supply of stemware, highball glasses, cordials, decanters, and cocktail napkins. And always consider lighting: a balanced mix of ambient, task, and decorative accent lighting is key for a glowing night-time dinner party.

WHY THIS ROOM WORKS

The combination of casual furniture, formal table settings, and dramatic displays gives this dining room an urbane sophistication.

■ **BLACK WALLS** signal a theatricality suitable to an entertaining space. The black backdrop puts glassware, white dinnerware, and silver in high relief.

■ **BLACKBOARD PAINT** on a section of wall lets the host announce the menu.

■ **A MIRRORED DRINKS CABINET** continues the storage-as-display theme and adds lustre to the setting.

■ **LIGHTING AT EVERY LEVEL** includes pendant lights set on a dimmer, recessed lights in the shelving and the Victorian dresser, and votive candles on the table. Reflective accessories enhance the flickering candlelight.

This open room with its soaring vistas makes a wonderful location for entertaining, offering plenty of space for food and beverage set-ups and room to mix and mingle.

■ THE BUFFET TABLE is set in the open and allows access from either side, so it can serve a large group efficiently.

■ A SELF-SERVICE BAR is set apart from the buffet table on a sturdy built-in bookcase, out of the flow of traffic.

■ COMFORTABLE SEATING is arranged throughout the room and out on the veranda. Generous armchairs and a sofa flank the fireplace.

■ DINING PLATES are set at one end of the table and cutlery at the other, to ensure smooth traffic flow.

■ BUNDLED CUTLERY is easier than separate pieces to carry from the table to a comfortable seat. Lash bundles together with a decorative tie.

■ MINIATURE PLAYING CARDS, tied with a loop of twine, help guests keep track of which wine glass is theirs.

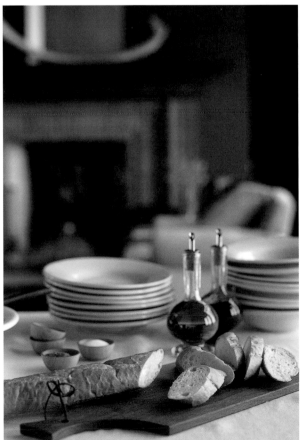

ENTERTAINING WITH STYLE

Buffet Style

Buffet-style dining is one of the easiest ways to entertain a crowd. The key to success lies in arranging the room to ease traffic flow.

Nearly everyone has occasions when they want to invite more guests than they have room for at their dining table. The simplest solution is to set up a buffet in the largest space in your house – it doesn't have to be in the dining room. A long, wide table is always the best choice, especially when dressed simply to allow plenty of room for food and serving pieces. Make sure there's space around the table for guests to move comfortably. If possible, situate the table so that guests can help themselves to food from both sides. Arrange seating groups throughout the space to encourage mingling, pulling in chairs from other rooms as necessary, and provide small tables to set down drinks.

A Festive Scene

With a little ingenuity, you can host a large-scale dinner at home. All it takes is a creative approach to seating and a fun sense of style.

It may seem daunting to plan a large formal dinner, but it's possible to stylishly seat and serve a crowd with ease. Look for places in your home that could be turned into a temporary dining room – perhaps one end of the living room, or a wide hallway. To seat a large group comfortably, you obviously need a long table. A couple of good options are using multiple tables lined up and dressed as one, or hiring banquet tables. Or forgo a single table altogether and set up a number of small tables instead, to evoke the lighthearted atmosphere of a bistro. Borrow lightweight wooden chairs from other rooms and mix them in with your dining chairs, or hire the number you need to provide ample seating.

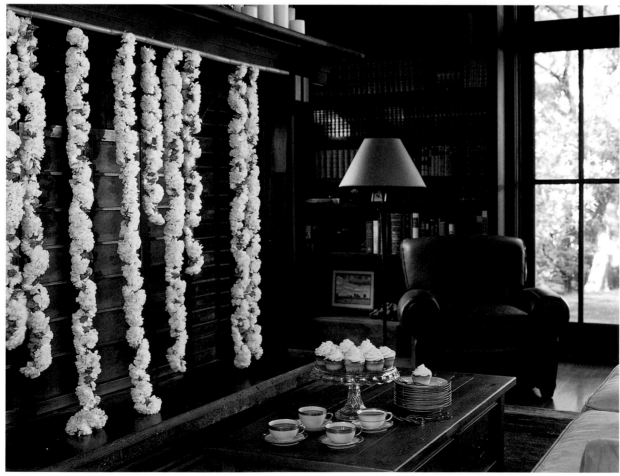

WHY THIS ROOM WORKS

A generous banquet table is fashioned from several square tables lined up, spanning the width of the room without crowding it. Because the table is narrow, this set-up takes up less space than you might think.

■ MIX-AND-MATCH CHAIRS provide sufficient seating while establishing a casual atmosphere.

■ A SEPARATE DESSERT AREA is set up in the adjoining study to encourage guests to mingle after the main meal.

■ SPECIAL TOUCHES greet guests from the moment they arrive. Murano glass cherries adorn the menus, and gift bags are tied to chairs. Portrait "place cards" are snapshots taken as guests arrive. Bottles of champagne, served in their own ice buckets with a straw, add a playful note.

■ CASUAL DECOR keeps the mood light for the festivities. A raw linen tablecloth signals informality, as do the loose and garlanded carnations used here in abundance.

FLOWERS FOR THE TABLE ARE EASY TO
STYLE WHEN YOU LET A SHAPELY CONTAINER
PROVIDE THE INSPIRATION, AND KEEP THE
CHOICE OF BLOSSOMS SIMPLE.

A small creamer, *above left*, holds a single
blossom, and one is put at each place setting.
Floral arrangements don't need to be set in the
middle of the table. This kind of individual
centrepiece is a nice way to make guests feel
special. Here the display also serves as a place
card, with the guest's name written directly on
the container. After the party, guests can take
their arrangements home.

Paper bags, *left*, are anything but prosaic when
painted in a variety of bold colours. The bags
make charming covers for an eclectic array of
containers. Each is filled with a generous bunch
of the same type of flower, and the painted
bags complement the flowers' hues without
overwhelming them.

A long, narrow vase, *above*, showcases the
sweet simplicity of tulips. The white ceramic
vase is low by design, adding colourful elegance
to a dining table without obstructing guests'
views. It's also a stylish choice for a mantel
or sideboard display. For dramatic impact
with minimal effort, choose just a single
variety of flower to fill a vase.

Showy alliums, *right*, standing in tall
glass containers make simple but striking
centrepieces that add dramatic impact to
the setting. To add colour high and low, rest
a few allium blooms directly on the table.
Here, glass pebbles, normally used as vase
fillers, are massed on the tablecloth to
create the effect of a luminous runner.

One of the most iconic and enduring images of home is that of the whole family gathered around a table, laughing and chatting while tucking into a lovingly prepared meal. It's not surprising, then, that the most popular gathering spot in many homes is the dining table. This is the stage on which everyday life is played out and reviewed, and one of the few places in our busy world where we can catch up with one another, pass time, and celebrate events large and small. Whether you

LAYING THE
FAMILY TABLE

THE DINING AREA IS OFTEN A HOUSE'S HOME BASE. MAKE IT A PLACE THAT SUITS YOUR NEEDS AND REFLECTS YOUR INTERESTS, AND IT WILL APPEAL TO FAMILY AND FRIENDS ALIKE.

have a compact kitchen–diner or a grand open-plan room, make sure that your dining area suits your family, reflects its style and interests, and can comfortably accommodate everything from holiday gatherings to game playing and bill paying. Hardwearing furnishings are a smart choice here. Choose durable furniture and tableware that can be easily dressed up for celebrations. Give the room the honour it deserves by decorating it with the things that you and your family love, adding personality and warmth with collections and artwork. Change table settings and accents often to keep the space feeling fresh and in step with the seasons.

Seasonal Celebrations

When family and friends gather around the table, set a festive tone with colourful, easy-to-do decorations and co-ordinated accents.

Setting a special dinner table for an extended-family celebration doesn't require a formal set-up or unusual effort. Just look to the season's bounty for inspired decorating ideas. Start with place settings in white or neutral tones, which make a perfect backdrop for napkins, tablecloths, and stemware in seasonal colours.

Whether using the earthy hues of harvest time or the soft colours of spring, you can arrange centrepieces drawn from Nature's palette. Make loose seasonal arrangements of flowers, herbs, gourds, berries, or branches. Candles are always welcome, and a single piece of stemware at each place lends just the right amount of elegance to a special occasion.

WHY THIS ROOM WORKS

Dressed for a holiday feast, this table takes its cues from autumn colours at their peak. The table setting is simple, but the colourful accents and thoughtful decorative touches make this a celebration.

■ BASIC WHITE DINNERWARE offers great flexibility for changing table decor. Mixed with accent pieces, it keeps any palette fresh and inviting.

■ A SEASONAL CENTREPIECE of pumpkins and bittersweet branches is paired with clusters of pillar candles. The natural decorations are repeated on the buffet hutch.

■ A CHILDREN'S TABLE makes little ones feel special. Kids can sit down to their own version of the grown-ups' table, complete with durable deep-dish plates, white sketchpads for place mats, and a supply of crayons.

■ CREATIVE PLACE CARDS encourage conversation and conviviality, especially when they involve an after-dinner game or activity.

LAYING THE FAMILY TABLE

Home Base

An informal kitchen–diner decorated with casual style makes everyone feel at ease and welcome to linger at any time of day.

A kitchen–diner has a special appeal for family and friends alike. It's convenient for families because while Mum and Dad are preparing dinner, kids can finish their homework (and ask for help) before it's time to lay the table. It's great for casual entertaining, too, as guests gravitate towards a kitchen anyway, and there's plenty of room for them to relax and chat with the cook.

One approach to decorating a kitchen–diner is to make it as homely and cosy as possible. Give its decor the same level of attention that you would a "proper" dining room, but take advantage of its informality by making it more personal. Signal that this is "family central" with displays of favourite objects and mementos that invite comment and recollection. Set collections and family treasures (such as groupings of collectable pottery, an array of children's artwork, beach shells from a summer outing, souvenirs from family holidays) around the space to give it character and interest.

Storage Options

Your enjoyment of your dinnerware and serving pieces will last only as long as they retain their beauty, and that means making sure they get proper care and handling. You don't need to develop a whole new regimen, how-ever. Just follow some basic commonsense storage rules, and your dishes, stemware, cutlery, and serving pieces will stay beautiful for generations.

Whether you choose to display your treasures out in the open for easy access and dramatic style, or tucked away in cupboards for a streamlined look, the first consideration is adequate protection. The fragile surfaces of many dinnerware pieces require plenty of space to protect them from friction, and adequate wrapping or storage systems that ensure safekeeping. Items that see daily use such as cutlery, crockery, and sturdy glassware are best kept close at hand and can be stored more casually. Finer pieces like china, crystal, stemware, and silver call for special consideration.

A wall of open shelves, *right*, turns this hallway into a modern version of a butler's pantry. Adjustable shelves accommodate pieces of varying heights, and some are fitted with baskets for holding linen and cutlery. Baskets on high shelves hold less-used items.

DESIGN LESSON CARING FOR DINNERWARE

When the big celebration is over and it's time to put away your special serving pieces, linen, and cutlery, some special rules apply for the storage of pieces you don't use frequently.

Padded, zipped cases made for safekeeping fine china are available in various sizes. You can make your own storage boxes, lined with bubble wrap and divided into sections with cardboard, to hold odd-shaped items like gravy boats and terrines; be sure to use acid-free archival cardboard. Felt and foam are proven materials for protecting stacks of china. Dish protectors in various sizes are commercially available to insert between plates; you can also cut your own felt or polystyrene dividers to slide between dishes.

■ FINE CHINA should be washed by hand with a mild detergent (without bleach or lemon scent) before storage, and, if unused, should be taken out and washed annually. Never stack plates higher than 20 cm (8 in).

■ FINE LINEN should be laid flat, wrapped in acid-free paper, and rolled rather than folded, to prevent mould and permanent creases.

■ SILVER PIECES are best kept in drawers or boxes lined with special tarnish-preventing fabric, or wrapped in acid-free tissue (never in plastic, wool, felt, newspaper, or chamois leather) and stored in polyethylene bags.

■ CRYSTAL AND STEMWARE should be washed by hand in warm water with mild detergent. Store upright on shelves or in padded cases.

Shelf Storage, *far left*
A series of shallow shelves, adjusted to allow for the height of the glasses plus about 3 cm (1 in), make glasses easy to reach. Always place crystal stemware upright when stored on shelves.

Hanging Stemware, *left*
Wineglasses and stemware must be stored with care. Hanging wineglasses by their stems in a mounted rack helps keep the bowls free of dust.

Covered Displays

Neatly arranged rows of glassware, plates, and teacups become lovely additions to a room's decor when stored in china cupboards or wall cupboards with glass doors. On-view storage is appealing because so many dining essentials have beautiful shapes. What's more, built-in cupboards can be customized to fit unusual serving pieces.

Open Displays

"Floating" display shelves mounted over a sideboard keep everyday dining necessities close at hand for daily use, and make buffet-style service simple for larger gatherings. Add one or two mementos to your mix of dinnerware and glasses, and your storage solution doubles as an attractive dining room display.

Special cutlery, *right*
Place settings slipped into individual tarnish-proof fabric pockets, rolled and tied, simplify laying the table.

Everyday cutlery, *far right*
Stainless and other daily-use cutlery can be kept at the ready by simply displaying it in glasses or other attractive containers.

Food just seems to taste better when eaten out-of-doors. Take advantage of this fact by setting an inviting table on the deck, on a lawn under the trees, in a courtyard, or on a poolside patio. Entertaining outdoors is ideal because it lets you enjoy both the planning and the party. You can let Mother Nature do the big decorating, and focus instead on adding the special details that complement a natural setting – comfortable seating, a strikingly laid table, and dramatic lighting. Whether you

DINING
OUTDOORS

A DINING SPACE IN THE BACK GARDEN, ON A MOUNTAINSIDE, OR AT WATER'S EDGE IS NATURALLY APPEALING. LET NATURE TAKE CARE OF THE DECOR, AND MAKE COMFORT YOUR PRIORITY.

have a small urban balcony or a sprawling garden patio, you can easily make outdoor dining a habit throughout the warm season. Start by equipping your space with furnishings that stand up to the elements. Today's options for water-resistant furniture and fabrics are nearly boundless, and you can now enjoy indoor comfort and style in outdoor areas without worries about the weather forecast. Then, to ensure a relaxed, convivial mood (and to lighten your workload), serve food buffet- or family-style, asking guests to pass dishes among themselves. When there are new faces in the crowd, there's no better way to get conversation going.

A Lakeside Table

Few things are more relaxing than a meal taken by a lake on a sunny day. Keep it informal with casual settings and durable dishware.

Any meal shared at the water's edge is an instant invitation for guests – and the host – to relax. When it's time to lay the table, keep in step with the laid-back surroundings. Dress the table simply and casually, with a bright, breezy (and washable) cotton tablecloth and napkins, and use great-looking (and practical) acrylic glassware and durable enamelware.

One of the best ways to keep an outdoor party lively is to serve food buffet-style. Bring out a sideboard from indoors and lay food and refreshments on it, using sturdy dishes and serving utensils. The ideal spot is close to a kitchen window, which the cook can use as a pass-through to set out a hearty meal with ease.

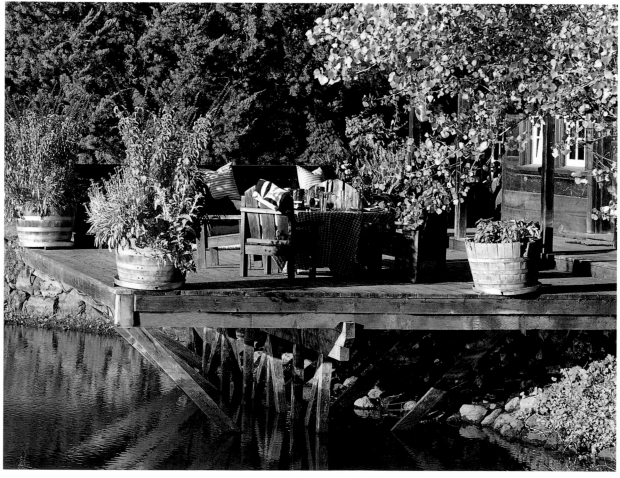

WHY THIS ROOM WORKS

A rustic lakefront dock outfitted with a durable outdoor dining set provides a mellow spot for summer meals. The style is laid-back and comfortable, encouraging everyone to relax and enjoy.

■ WEATHER-RESISTANT FURNISHINGS stand up to the elements and are ready for any gathering, whether dressed up for dinner or down for game playing.

■ A RED-AND-WHITE PALETTE, played out in solids, stripes, and plaids, keeps the mood light and adds punch to the natural surroundings.

■ CASUAL ACCESSORIES like printed cotton cushions and festive striped blankets add comfort to the solid, practical furniture. Kitchen towels serve as napkins.

■ A WINDOW SILL SHELF made from an old metal sign makes a convenient serving station. The cook can pass the food through the window for guests to serve themselves. This also makes tidying up more efficient.

WHY THIS ROOM WORKS

WHY THIS ROOM WORKS

In this poolhouse dining room, a calming palette of blue and white is played out in casual style to capture the sunny mood of long summer days.

■ **AN INDOOR–OUTDOOR MIX** of dining room luxuries and outdoor accoutrements provides comfort and invigorating freshness.

■ **AN OUTDOOR FIREPLACE** extends the season for dining out-of-doors.

■ **SEA COLOURS** are carried throughout the room, from the varying patterns of block-print pillows on the chairs to the laminated fabric place mats and durable acrylic tableware. The setting is quite simple but appears elegant.

■ **NAUTICAL THEMES** abound, including bookends used to hold napkins.

DINING OUTDOORS

Dinner by the Pool

A poolhouse or patio is a natural backdrop for summer get-togethers. Lay a colourful table by the water and guests will linger for hours.

If you're fortunate enough to have a swimming pool, a dining area that's set in a poolhouse or on a poolside patio is the perfect spot for a whole season of outdoor entertaining. In such an appealing setting, not a lot of fuss is required, so you can keep things relatively simple and spend more time conversing with your guests.

Start with a summery table set for enjoying the easy pleasures of a barbecue or seafood risotto. Durable wicker furniture, now available in a wide range of colours, naturally evokes a warm-weather mood. Set wicker chairs around the table, and make them comfortable with weatherproof cushions. Create a sea-side mood by outfitting the table in sailing colours and nautical stripes. In the summer sun, blue accents used in furnishings and tableware evoke the ocean and the deep azure of the sky at dusk. If you don't have a covered deck, be sure to keep patio umbrellas on hand for protection from direct sun or summer showers.

A Country Setting

To add a personal touch to an outdoor meal, establish a theme based on the location, and follow it through with witty details.

Once you've found the perfect spot to spend a sunny afternoon with great friends and good food, look to the setting itself for the party's style. When you adopt a theme that's in sync with the surroundings, it's easier to put together a memorable gathering. Centre your table decor around one idea – a casual harvest luncheon, an elegant lawn party. Find flowers, foliage, and branches that grow nearby to create simple centrepieces. Instead of using indoor dining chairs, scout out other options. If lunch is in the park, pull a table up to benches; if it's behind a barn, set up hay bales for seating. When it comes to food and drinks, make it easy on yourself by using disposable containers to cut down on tidying up.

WHY THIS ROOM WORKS

A country-theme dinner set on the sunny side of a barn fits seamlessly into the landscape. Everything from the seating and table coverings to the centrepieces are inspired by the locale.

■ HAY BALE BENCHES flanking the long table are a clever seating alternative; paintbrushes at each setting double as witty clothes brushes for loose straw.

■ THE HESSIAN TABLECLOTH is large enough to cover the legs of a hired folding table. A narrow length of raw linen frames the centrepieces, and small kitchen towels are used as napkins.

■ THEMED DETAILS, including a wheelbarrow ice chest and camping lanterns hung from rakes, set a lighthearted mood. Wildflowers are picked in bunches and set directly in simple glass containers – no arranging necessary.

■ TAKE-AWAY CONTAINERS serve as easy-care dishware and simplify food service and cleaning up.

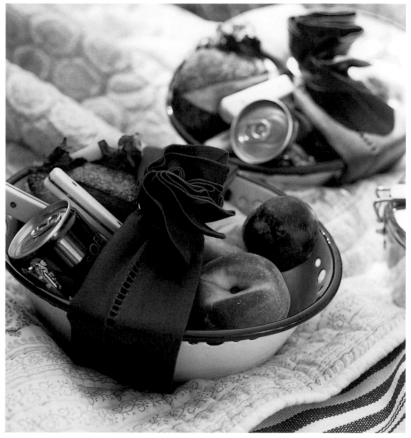

BRING STYLE OUTDOORS WITH
AN EASY MENU AND PORTABLE FOOD
PRESENTATIONS THAT SIMPLIFY SERVING
MEALS IN A FRESH-AIR SETTING.

An antique bottle caddy, *opposite top,* makes it a breeze to whisk dessert out to the table. Glass tumblers set in each compartment hold waffle cones, filled with fresh fruit and wrapped in striped napkins. This serving idea has a nostalgic appeal that captures the magic of childhood summers at the beach.

Bundled sandwiches, *opposite bottom,* are neatly wrapped with paper napkins and bound with twine. A length of matching twine is all you need to tie together cutlery. This portable serving system lets guests easily help themselves and can be prepared before a party.

Twine-tied rocks, *left,* anchor a tablecloth in case a breeze kicks up at a waterfront table. Table anchors can be crafted from found objects such as large seashells or smooth river stones. Tie a row of stones together with a continuous length of string, as shown here, to make them more manageable.

Enamelled bowls, *above,* corral individual lunches into a neat package, complete with cutlery and a drink. The easy-to-assemble contents are held in place with a napkin, which also functions as a convenient handle, so the bowls can be carried to the garden or picnic area.

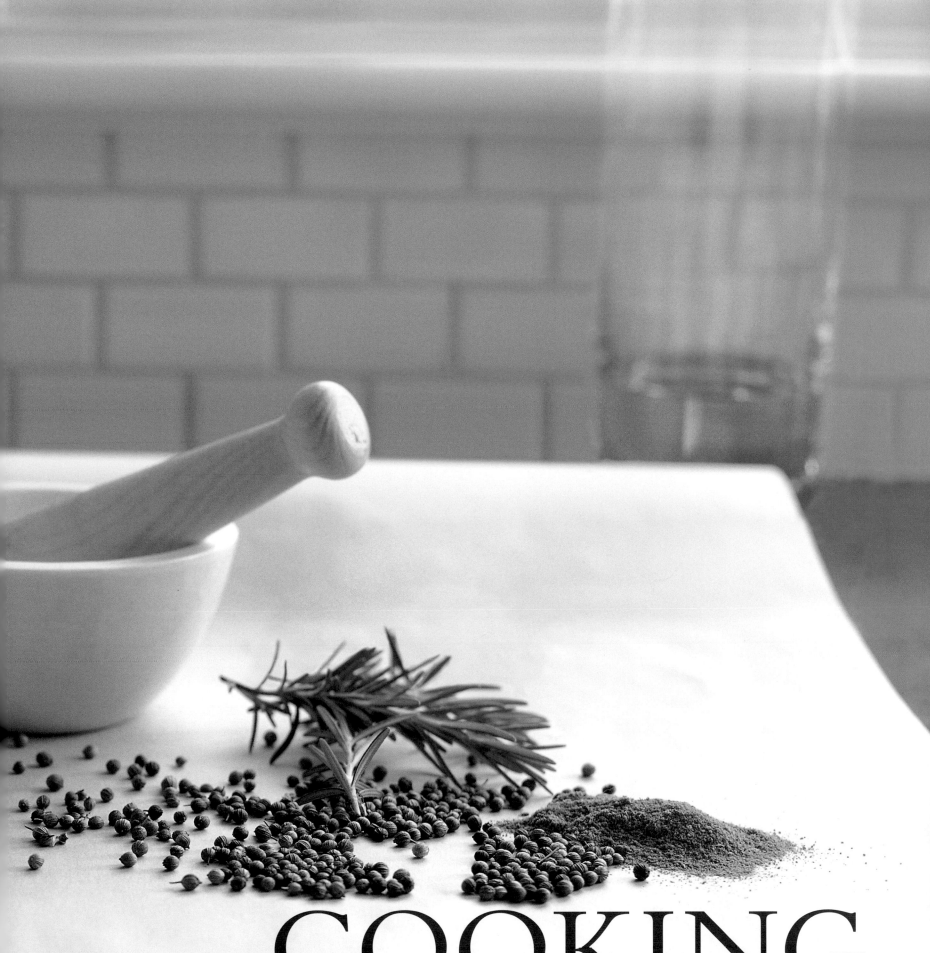

COOKING

"THE KITCHEN REALLY IS THE HEART OF MY HOME. THIS IS MY FAVOURITE PLACE BECAUSE EVERYONE GATHERS HERE, AND I CAN CATCH UP WITH FAMILY AND FRIENDS AS I COOK."

ELEMENTS OF A SUCCESSFUL
KITCHEN

The kitchen has come into its own as a living space. Kitchens have always been essential to home life, but these days we spend more time in them and use them for a wider range of activities than ever before. Besides being larger and more open than other rooms of the home, the kitchen is now looking more like the rest of the house, incorporating elements like wood flooring, cupboards designed to resemble furniture, and decorative accessories such as art and culinary collections. At the same time, this space is becoming more customized, with appliances and conveniences that are as forward-thinking as anything available for the home.

For the following pages, we've selected a number of rooms that demonstrate the latest ideas in making a kitchen hardworking and relaxing, well-planned and full of warmth.

How to Plan a Kitchen

In the kitchen, functional considerations that affect how the space works are more vital to your initial planning than style decisions. Begin by establishing an efficient work triangle, the key to every well-planned kitchen.

Time-tested guidelines offer useful parameters for a well-designed kitchen. Always start with the work triangle. Simply put, the work triangle is defined by the placement of the sink, cooker or hob, and refrigerator. An efficient work triangle minimizes how far you must walk while preparing a meal. Ideally, each leg of the triangle measures between 1.2–3 m (4–9 ft) and the sum of the three sides of the triangle should be between 5–8 m (16–26 ft). These dimensions also accommodate the minimum amount of worktop and

storage space you'll need. The sink area ideally will include 60 cm (24 in) of under-worktop space for a dishwasher, and you should allow 75–120 cm (30–48 in) of worktop surface between the sink and the cooker, which is the area where you'll spend the bulk of your time while cooking.

If two cooks regularly use your kitchen simultaneously, plan a second food preparation area around another sink, usually set in a centre island. Including an island or peninsula in your plan provides more workspace for two cooks and keeps the work triangle outside the family's traffic paths (see opposite page for more about islands). Because the refrigerator is used frequently by family members between meals, it's best to position it at the outside edge of the workspace, so it can be easily accessed whether you're cooking or simply snacking.

FAMILY KITCHEN

This room (above and preceding page) features an oversize island that has an attached kitchen table incorporated into its design. The table is the family communication centre as well as a place to dine together.

■ THE EFFICIENT WORK TRIANGLE is removed from traffic, thanks to a stainless steel sink in the work end of the island.

■ A LARGE FARMHOUSE-STYLE sink sits well out of the way of food preparation, so kids and other non-cooks can use it easily.

■ WORKTOP HEIGHTS are varied for different tasks; the table top is 76 cm (30 in) high, the standard for dining and also a baker's dream: the ideal counter height for kneading dough is 71–81 cm (28–32 in).

■ WORKTOP AND STORAGE SPACE is maximized in this L-shaped configuration.

FAMILY ROOM

UTILITY CUPBOARD

DINING ROOM

U-SHAPED KITCHEN-DINER

This combination kitchen–dining area is organized in a U-shaped plan, one of the most efficient possibilities because it results in long stretches of worktop surface and cupboard storage.

The main food preparation area has a generous 1.2 m (4 ft) length of worktop space.

The work triangle is out of the way of foot traffic passing through the room.

An oval table is a good choice to visually enlarge a small dining area, as its rounded corners take up less space.

Groceries may be unloaded on the island, within reach of both cupboards and refrigerator.

Each aisle is 105 cm (42 in) wide, the minimum distance needed within a cooking area.

OPEN GALLEY

The biggest drawback of a galley kitchen – the feeling of a tight enclosure – is eliminated when the kitchen is part of an open-plan space. Use common materials throughout all areas to integrate the kitchen seamlessly.

Where a sofa might be an awkward fit, three easy chairs provide generous seating.

PATIO

ENTRANCE

A galley kitchen with an island is cook-friendly, as the work triangle is compact and nothing is far from reach.

A walk-in cupboard maximizes storage and sits outside the work triangle, next to the refrigerator.

A TV cupboard in the living area is crafted in a similar style and material as the kitchen cupboards, to help unify the open plan.

When extra chairs are needed for dining, armchairs can be brought over from this seating area.

KITCHEN ISLANDS

Islands are an efficient way to add extra storage and work surface to your kitchen. If the island includes a sink or hob, it can tighten the work triangle and save steps.

Island Size
Ideal dimensions for islands call for a 90-cm (3-ft) high worktop that is at least 66 cm (25 in) deep. A breakfast bar may be taller than the worktop side. It should be 1.2 m (4 ft) high to fit stools for seating, and at least 36 cm (14 in) deep.

36 cm (14 in) 66 cm (25 in)

1.2 m (4 ft) 90 cm (3 ft)

Room Size
A kitchen island requires a room that's at least 2.4 x 3.5 m (8 x 12 ft) to accommodate it comfortably.

Efficiency
If you have two cooks in the family, it's helpful to have two sinks, one located in the island, to help establish dual preparation areas.

Materials
You can use materials on the island that match or complement the cupboards, but many cooks choose ones that differ from surrounding worktops. If you enjoy baking, opt for a marble worktop to keep dough cool and workable. Or go with something totally different. A free-standing farmhouse table or a stainless steel worktable used as an island can form an intriguing centrepiece.

Customized Storage
Capitalize on storage space within an island by fitting deeper shelves that hold bowls and pots on the cooking side, and shallow shelves for glassware on the dining side. Open storage under an island is a great place for appliances and bulky cookware that won't fit in standard cupboards.

Smart planning is the first step of any design, and this is especially true in the kitchen. This is a space that has to look and feel as inviting as the rest of your rooms and yet work harder than any of them. Above all, it's essential that your kitchen works *for you*. Fortunately, there are so many options for customizing a kitchen these days that everyone can benefit from new designs. Start by looking at how you'll use the space. Are you a gourmet cook, or does your busy lifestyle mean that you rely more

DESIGNING
YOUR DREAM KITCHEN

THE BEST KITCHENS ARE EFFICIENT HOME BASES FOR COOKING, RELAXING, AND ENTERTAINING. MAKE YOURS A JOY TO COME HOME TO AND A PLEASURE TO WORK IN.

on prepared foods? A perfect kitchen affords comfort and ease for all the things you do most often. If you and your family like to cook together, make sure you have plenty of room for separate work zones, and think about installing an extra sink. If you enjoy entertaining, perhaps an open-plan space is best, so you can be part of the fun while preparing the food. This could be the time to add a pantry, breakfast bar, or laundry cupboard; install dual dishwashers or a wine cupboard; or get that kitchen work desk you've always wanted. Dream big, then plan carefully. Kitchens demand more detailed decisions than other rooms, but the results are worth it.

The New Classic

Built for efficiency and easy upkeep, the service kitchens of yesterday's grand estates hold valuable design lessons for today's spaces.

For a state-of-the-art kitchen, look to the past. White cupboards, glazed underground tiles, stone worktops, and stainless steel fittings are design elements that recall the servants' kitchens of historic estates. These materials make good sense for use in today's family kitchen for the same reason they were favoured then: durability. Overscale work islands, another key element in estate kitchens, allow multiple cooks to work together comfortably. A second sink installed in the island can tighten the work triangle, saving steps for the cook. Pantries, once the norm, are also making a comeback. A pantry's great advantage is that it offers efficient storage with fewer cupboards, so there's room for more windows, an asset in any kitchen.

WHY THIS ROOM WORKS

This generously proportioned kitchen combines classic materials with up-to-date amenities and is as stylish as it is practical.

■ AN OVERSIZE ISLAND anchors the expansive space and provides an enviable work surface. Its open base offers a great deal of accessible storage on all sides but minimizes its bulk.

■ A U-SHAPED LAYOUT creates an efficient work triangle (a refrigerator, not visible, is to the right of the hob). A second sink, fitted in the island, diminishes the size of the triangle and puts it outside the main traffic aisle.

■ A WALK-IN PANTRY behind the hob wall diminishes the number of cupboards needed, freeing one wall for a bank of windows.

■ CO-ORDINATED ACCENT MATERIALS and accessories in tin and in black and white add to the room's handsome appeal. A custom-made spice cupboard, centred within the hob niche, adds a simple and useful focal point.

Smart Choices for the Home Chef

If you love to cook and want a more efficient and satisfying place to prepare meals, outfit your kitchen with features favoured by the pros.

Commercial kitchens are the domain of professional chefs, but they offer ideas that you can borrow to enhance your own kitchen. Appliances with the power and efficiency of those found in restaurant kitchens are widely available in versions adapted for the home, and some modifications to kitchen materials can be made without requiring a total renovation. Choose features that suit your preferred style of cooking. For example, a marble worktop keeps pastry dough cool and firm; a tap at the cooker makes fast work of filling pots for soups or seafood boils; an island sink simplifies rinsing vegetables before chopping and tidying up afterwards.

WHY THIS ROOM WORKS

Centred around an island worktable, this kitchen for an avid cook incorporates appliances and customized storage solutions adopted from professional kitchens.

■ A RESTAURANT-STYLE COOKER is fitted with a water line and a long-necked spigot for filling pots; a rail keeps frequently used utensils organized and accessible.

■ AMPLE STORAGE is on every level, with spaces customized for specific items. Chilled wine is conveniently located in a refrigerated wine cupboard; a customized drawer keeps jars of spices organized.

■ SMALL APPLIANCES such as the mixer and toaster are home-sized versions of professional models. They deliver the power and ease of their commercial counterparts.

■ A BUILT-IN OFFICE NOOK offers a worktop for recipe planning. Shelves above hold cookery books, food magazines, and other kitchen items.

WHY THIS ROOM WORKS

This kitchen feels more spacious than its actual size, thanks to its open styling. A peninsula serves as a food preparation area, sideboard, and gathering spot.

■ SIMPLE MATERIALS and fixtures blend with well-edited collections to create a casual look.

■ A LARGE WINDOW floods the room with natural light, which bounces off the bright surfaces and gleaming stainless steel. Butcher-block worktops lend the sunny space warmth.

■ VINTAGE GLASS CANISTERS and jars of different shapes and sizes allow the cook to easily see what's inside and also make a pleasing decorative grouping.

■ PERSONAL COLLECTIONS lining the shelves give the room character.

DESIGNING YOUR DREAM KITCHEN

Easy Entertaining

If you're a cook who tends towards simple meals and take-aways, you're free to enjoy the pleasures of a pared-down, open-style space.

For the occasional cook, an open kitchen tucked into a small space can be just what's wanted for informal entertaining and dining. Even a small kitchen can be a relaxing place to cook and congregate when the essentials are all right at hand. Keep frequently used ingredients and utensils at the cook's fingertips, and incorporate a peninsula or island into the design to allow the host and guests to carry on a conversation while preparing the food. A butcher-block–topped open worktop is versatile, too. It's roomy enough to chop on and beautiful enough to serve hors d'oeuvres from at a cocktail party. It also makes a perfect sideboard for spreading out food to serve buffet-style.

Open shelves may replace overhead cupboards, leaving collections and dishware on view and expanding the room's sense of space. Using a monochromatic palette and straightforward materials like stainless steel and butcher block keeps a kitchen feeling uncluttered.

Making the most of space is a different challenge in every room. It may mean enjoying a wealth of space and customizing it for maximum comfort. It also might mean making creative use of every possible inch to provide adequate work space and increase storage potential. Whatever size room you have, it requires good space planning. In a kitchen, this means addressing two major concerns. First, there's a need to create well-designed work zones (for preparation, cooking, cleaning

MAXIMIZING
YOUR KITCHEN SPACE

FROM THE LARGEST ROOM TO THE SMALLEST CUPBOARD, ANY SPACE BENEFITS FROM A SMART SYSTEM. THE KEY TO A WELL-RUN KITCHEN IS THOUGHTFUL SPACE PLANNING.

up, and storage) and an efficient work triangle (the set-up of the refrigerator, cooker, and sink in relation to one another). A well-thought-out floor plan provides all of this so that your kitchen will run smoothly. The other essential in any kitchen is abundant storage. This is best achieved with a combination of inventive storage aids: variable-height shelving and compartmentalized drawers, corner lazy Susans, baking trays and tray racks, pull-out shelves and baskets – the options are almost endless. All these features can be added to existing cupboards, too, so you don't need to plan a whole-room remodel to take advantage of their efficiencies.

WHY THIS ROOM WORKS

Functioning as both kitchen and dining room, this generous space is a favourite place to gather and linger for snacks or large dinners.

■ **THE KITCHEN WORK AREA** is laid out with a small work triangle for optimal ease and efficiency.

■ **THE CENTRE ISLAND** has a dining bar built into one side, offering a spot for snacks or light meals or for guests to gather while meals are prepared.

■ **AN ANTIQUE CUPBOARD** in the dining area keeps china and linen close at hand, and brings the warmth and personality often associated with other rooms into the kitchen space.

■ **BUTLER'S PANTRY–STYLE CUPBOARDS** and half-panelled walls give a vintage look to the open space.

MAXIMIZING YOUR KITCHEN SPACE

The Kitchen–Diner

Bring together the pleasures of cooking, eating, and entertaining with a hardworking kitchen that incorporates a roomy, graceful dining area.

Estate agent listings herald a "kitchen–diner" for good reason. Many families covet a kitchen–dining room set-up that can be used for gatherings great and small. Such a plan retains the warmth that is among a kitchen-diner's best assets but adds an uncommon sense of spaciousness. By combining a kitchen and dining room, you can bring a greater feeling of flow to your home's layout. It also allows you to allocate different areas to different kinds of dining. Weekday breakfasts, informal lunches, and quick meals can be served at a dining bar designed as part of a kitchen island; family suppers and dinner parties may be enjoyed at a large table in the dedicated dining area. A centre island is ideal for entertaining, as it allows guests to gather during meal preparation and lets the cook feel like part of the party even while working. For the most harmonious effect, the kitchen and dining decor should complement each other but be subtly different, as befits their purposes.

A Ship-Shape Galley

Give a narrow kitchen all the advantages of a larger one. Smart planning makes a galley kitchen a room that's a pleasure to work in.

A galley kitchen – which takes its name from ships' galleys, where space is notoriously tight – is one of the realities of many urban homes and flats. Though a galley kitchen may not be terribly spacious, it can be wonderfully efficient. One of its greatest assets is the compact size of its work triangle, which ensures that nothing is ever far from the cook's reach and makes the room an enjoyable workspace. One common disadvantage is a lack of space for storage, but this can be remedied. Specialized cupboards like pull-out pantry towers, shallow pantry-style cupboards, and custom-built drawers make use of every inch; special appliances in smaller-than-normal sizes take up less space.

WHY THIS ROOM WORKS

This galley kitchen is quite narrow, but it gives the illusion of being larger due to its all-white colour palette. Materials and textures are limited to just a few, and the worktops are kept uncluttered, further enhancing an open feel.

■ AN OPTIMAL WORK TRIANGLE is achieved in the small room: cooker, sink, and refrigerator (on the wall opposite the cooker) are all within easy reach of the cook.

■ SHALLOW WALL CUPBOARDS are not the standard 30–38 cm (12–15 in) deep, but instead are pantry-style, just deep enough for one row of items. Because of their shallow depth, they're able to be flush-mounted to avoid any overhang of the worktop below.

■ A WALL-MOUNTED TAP saves precious inches, further enhancing the streamlined look of the room.

■ HIDDEN DRAWERS behind white cupboard doors preserve the room's clean-lined effect.

Creative Storage

The best ways to use space aren't always merely functional. Be clever about using the space you have and bring style to storage.

One of the most crucial elements of space planning in the kitchen is storage. Nearly everyone wishes they had more of it, customized to fit every cooking item. With a little ingenuity, you can create more room for storage and give your kitchen a personalized look at the same time. Begin by customizing every space you can. Subdivide storage compartments with decorative trays, baskets, bowls, and racks. Put items that you use every day like napkins and cutlery into a basket and leave it in a spot convenient to the dining table. Where there's room, make decorative displays of produce or other common necessities. Corral cooking oils and vinegars in a rimmed tray and leave it out on the worktop.

WHY THIS ROOM WORKS

This spacious kitchen with its generous centre island features a combination of fixed and movable storage containers, offering a multitude of flexible options.

■ **OPEN AND CLOSED STORAGE** compartments are designed into the island, allowing easy access to frequently used essentials but concealing less often used items.

■ **BASKETS WITH CUT-OUT HANDLES** form an orderly grid that conceals towels, snacks, and spices.

■ **FLEA-MARKET TREASURES** are repurposed for storage: a bottle drying rack is pressed into service as a cup holder.

■ **DECORATIVE TRAYS** keep hard-to-organize items like cutlery and condiments neat and portable.

■ **THE CASUAL DECOR** of warm wooden cupboards, salvaged wooden beams, and a rustic metal vent hood are a handsome backdrop for the unique collectables on display.

Cupboard Options

Your choice of cupboards defines your kitchen's style, so it's often the first consideration after establishing a space plan. Whether you prefer open or closed cupboards or a mix of both, the range of choices is tremendous, with each style offering different material, frame, and finish options. Face-frame cupboards, whose doors have a raised frame around the centre panel, are more classic; frameless cupboards are completely flat-fronted and afford a more streamlined look. Stock cupboards save money, though they offer fewer choices in style. With so many organizing systems available, stock cupboards can be easily fitted with custom-made storage accessories. Semi-customized cupboards offer more diverse finishes as well as superior materials and construction. Fully customized cupboards offer high-end details like self-closing drawers, pull-out drawers, spice or knife drawers, and toe-kick drawers – the options are almost endless. For more information, see Materials, page 360.

Wooden lower cupboards, *right*, are paired with stainless steel shelves to make efficient and attractive use of this wall. A mix of open and closed storage options is a clever way to put attractive items on view while keeping more utilitarian pieces behind doors.

DESIGN LESSON PANTRY STORAGE

It used to be that pantries were separate rooms off the kitchen, designed to contain every ingredient that a cook needed. Today, the definition of a pantry has expanded to include built-in towers or free-standing cupboards, often customized with an array of special storage fittings. Within a tall storage unit, shelves pull out or are only the depth of one can or box, so all your stored supplies are visible at a glance. Not only can you spot things quickly, there's no need to move things out from the front to get to items in the back. Pantries don't have to be large to be efficient, and they can be carved out of over-looked spaces, too, such as underneath a stairway, along the walls of the basement stairs, or in an underused kitchen corner.

■ TAKE ADVANTAGE OF FITTINGS like door ladders, swing-out or pull-out baskets and shelves, and lazy Susans, to make maximum use of pantry space. The ability to pull items out towards you is essential in deep cupboards, where items at the back are difficult to access.

■ DOOR-MOUNTED SHELVES add efficiency to a pantry space. All shelving fitted here should have a lip or restraint on the front to prevent items from falling off when the door is opened or closed.

■ CREATE SEPARATE ZONES for different items – canned goods, baking ingredients, packaged foods, etc. – to make it easier to find what you need and stay organized.

Glass-Front Doors, *right*
Doors with glass panes appeal for different reasons. Some people like the look of turn-of-the-century butler's pantry cupboards, which commonly had multiple panes of glass; some cooks just like to see their well-filled larders. Glass doors also help a small kitchen appear larger.

Translucent Doors, *far right*
Semiopaque panes on cupboards are a distinctive way to let light into a kitchen. Here, frosted glass doors are mounted in front of a window, maximizing both light and storage. Bowls and vases are silhouetted by the outside light in a unique abstract presentation.

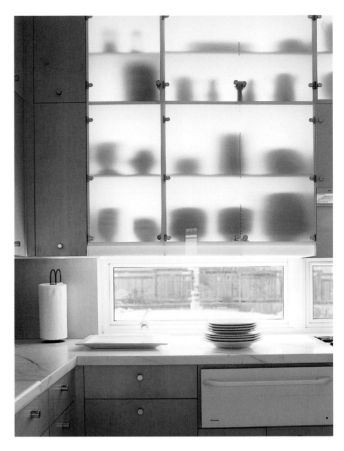

Wood, *right*
Lumber remains the top choice for kitchen cupboards. Wood not only is durable, but also can be easily stained, painted, or glazed to suit any decor. Frames, panels, and moulding add character for a traditional look; frameless wood can be quite contemporary.

Laminate, *far right*
Laminated cupboards have an up-to-date appeal that can be striking when paired with warm wood flooring or furniture. Laminates require less care than wood and are stain- and scuff-resistant. Vinyl and laminate cupboards are available in even more varieties than wood, in matt, textured, and gloss finishes.

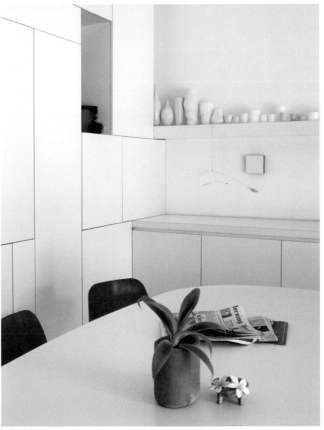

Pull-Out Shelves

Fitting low cupboards or a pantry with pull-out shelves saves you having to bend or squat to remove things. Sliding trays similar to this one can be retrofitted into existing cupboards for a modest cost. Their drawer-like construction prevents objects from sliding off when the shelf is being rolled in or out.

Deep Drawers

A deep drawer keeps things more accessible than a deep shelf does because items located at the back can be found and taken out more easily. Drawer storage of bottles works best when the drawer is divided into sections and each section is fairly full. This helps prevent bottles from shifting and toppling.

Under-Appliance Drawer

A shallow drawer built under an appliance or cupboard is a great example of efficient use of space. This one, tucked under a cooker, is perfectly situated for corralling baking sheets and assorted tins and moulds. Toe-kick drawers can be installed to capitalize on space under almost any cupboard, and there are even folding stepladders that fit in a toe-kick space.

Pegboard Dividers

A pegboard system provides flexible options for organizing drawers. Push pegs into the holes to separate and steady items. This adjustable storage solution works for virtually any kind of object – stacks of dishes and teacups, spice jars, linen, cooking implements – whatever you may need to organize in your drawers.

Island Storage

Make the most of space within a kitchen island by incorporating both deep and shallow storage into it. On the cooking side, 60 cm (24 in-deep) cupboards hide large cooking equipment. On the dining side, shallow shelves utilize space that might otherwise be wasted. A colourful display of tableware brightens and personalizes this island.

Adjustable Shelves

Installing adjustable shelves or slide-out drawers inside cupboards is a simple and inexpensive way to tailor storage to your specific needs and accommodate assorted sizes of cookware. Allow 3–8 cm (1–3 in) of space between the tallest item and the next shelf, to facilitate moving items in and out.

Under-Worktop Storage Options

The areas under your worktops are usually the largest storage spaces in your kitchen. To maximize space and keep it organized, customize the shelves, drawers, or racks to suit your needs. There are many ready-made fittings now available that you can install in existing cupboards to replace or add to fixed shelves. Fit roll-out shelves into deep cupboards to make it simpler to find what you need; add dividers to deep drawers, sectioning them into quadrants; attach racks to the insides of cupboard doors. Use adjustable shelving, and set the shelves at heights customized for specific contents. Group like items by size and by task, then keep groups nearest their work zone – pots near the cooker, oils near the prep area, towels and sponges next to the tidy-up zone, and so on. Assign a spot to every item in the kitchen, and you'll never wonder where anything has gone.

Open shelves beneath the cooker, *left*, are the perfect spot for pots and pans, providing quick access to them for the cook. Heavy-duty shelving can also hold small appliances, freeing up worktop space.

DESIGN LESSON ADJUST THE HEIGHT TO FIT

While specialized built-in storage is one of the benefits of custom-designed cupboards, another increasingly popular advantage is the ability to adjust the height of the worktop to fit the cook. All standard base cupboards are 90 cm (36 in) high, a comfortable working height for the general population. Taller cooks can install cupboards that bring the work surface up to as high as 114 cm (45 in), eliminating straining and awkward bending at the worktop. Cooks come in all sizes, and recent research into repetitive-stress injuries and ergonomics indicates that the best work surfaces vary in height depending on the task. Besides adjusting worktop height, you may also want to modify shelf and wall-oven installations for maximum comfort.

■ WORKTOP HEIGHT: Chopping, kneading dough, and mixing by hand are more comfortable on a surface that is 70–80 cm (28–32 in) high. Many cooks instinctively move to a table, whose height allows them to fully extend their arms while working.

■ OVEN PLACEMENT: The bottom of a wall oven should not be higher than waist level, to avoid burning your arms on the open door as you remove a heated dish.

■ STORAGE HEIGHT: Shelves and cupboards between your knee and eye-level are the ones you can most comfortably reach without stretching. It's not practical to limit storage to that area, but use this guideline for storing things you use often.

eye-level: maximum height for often-used storage.

up to 114 cm (45 in) worktop height is better for taller cooks.

90 cm (36 in): standard cupboard height.

70–80 cm (28–32 in): best for chopping, kneading dough, or mixing.

For most people, the kitchen is the hub around which the whole family revolves. So it makes sense that the decor of a kitchen should reflect the tastes and interests of the family it serves. There's no denying that care for decorative items is a concern here, since cooking and cleaning can be damaging to delicate pieces. Turn this fact to your advantage and tell your style story in ways that are uniquely appropriate to this space. This means decorating with items that are beautifully durable. The

EXPRESSING
YOUR STYLE

THE KITCHEN IS ONE OF A HOME'S MOST ESSENTIAL SPACES. ENHANCE YOURS WITH COLLECTIONS AND TREASURES THAT SPEAK VOLUMES ABOUT YOU AND YOUR FAMILY.

most obvious first choice is culinary-related pieces. Everyday items like cookery books, crockery, servingware, and flavoured vinegars are naturals for kitchen displays. Collectables like vintage linen, salt and pepper shakers, biscuit jars and canisters, or antique kitchen tools also have great visual appeal. If you have a number of collections, you can rearrange or swap them for a quick change of style in the room. Plants are another smart option. Herbs can be grown in pots or boxes, trimmed as topiaries, or dried and hung. And children's artwork is always a favourite choice, bringing warmth and whimsy to this family-oriented space.

WHY THIS ROOM WORKS

This open-plan dining room and kitchen has an appealing flow to its space, good definition of zones, and a cohesive sense of style.

■ THE ISLAND WORKTOP is higher on the dining side and lower on the food preparation side, so it conceals worktops from diners.

■ AN OPEN HANGING PLATE RACK above the island completes the see-through "wall" separating the two areas.

■ CONSISTENT COLOURS AND MATERIALS are used throughout the space, and a red accent colour is seen repeatedly throughout the zones.

■ A NATURAL WOVEN RUG defines the dining and lounging areas.

■ LARGE-SCALE WINDOWS expand the space and flood all areas with sunlight.

EXPRESSING YOUR STYLE

An Open Approach

Create a sense of harmony in an open-plan room by maintaining a continuity of style that reflects the beauty of the rest of your home.

You have no doubt seen and read a lot about open-plan spaces, or "great rooms". These multi-purpose rooms offer countless possibilities for configuring the ways you cook, dine, and entertain. The first step in making an open-plan kitchen and dining area work is to look at the space as a whole rather than approaching it as two different rooms. Strive to bring to it the overall style of your home. Give it a cohesive look by using the same flooring and other materials in both areas, and paint the walls the same colour – or carry an accent colour from one area to the next. Subtly suggest division between the spaces in ways that maintain a sense of openness. Use beams or other architectural markers, hanging pot- or plate racks, furniture placement, or area rugs to indicate zones. This is important if your plan includes a living room. The more space you have, the more it needs to be shaped to create functional areas that display your style.

Simply White

An all-white kitchen is a fresh and bright decorating choice that delivers dramatic impact with understated, elegant style.

Sometimes the best way to make a strong statement is with silence. The same is true in decorating. An absence of colour can make as strong a personal declaration as a showy abundance of it. An all-white color scheme also has the benefit of feeling fresh, clean, and bright, qualities that are especially desirable in a kitchen. The best complement for an all-white room is a wealth of natural light, which enlivens any space. Leave windows uncovered, or partially covered with sheers or bottom-mount blinds, to maximize sunlight streaming in. Mix shades of white in matt and gloss surfaces with clear glass pieces, and combine various shapes, textures, and patterns to give the room warmth and dynamism.

WHY THIS ROOM WORKS

A pure white colour scheme, carried out in everything from the furnishings to the trim and tableware, makes this kitchen feel fresh and especially soothing.

■ HIGH-GLOSS PAINT transforms a simple wooden dining set into a striking furnishing choice.

■ SUBSTANTIAL SHELVES and brackets provide welcome architectural detail on an otherwise plain wall.

■ MATERIALS AND FIXTURES are practical and modest, yet convey a sense of elegance due to the calm harmony of hues.

■ OPEN STORAGE suits the simple and casual aesthetic of the room.

■ A TABLEWARE COLLECTION of mixed contemporary and antique pieces adds texture and interest to the room. The cool and warm tones of the white and transparent pieces give the arrangement movement and visual variety.

BRING PERSONAL TOUCHES INTO YOUR KITCHEN WITH ART, FAMILY PHOTOS, AND COLLECTIONS THAT ADD WHIMSY AND CHARACTER.

Antique graters, *opposite top*, hang in the empty space on the side of a cupboard. Unique collections often spark conversation in the kitchen. Every favourite object holds a story about its origin, whether a memorable family trip or just a day wandering a flea market.

A corkboard, *opposite bottom*, fitted with colourful drawing pins, makes a decorative statement. Covered with family photos, mementos, invitations, and postcards, it becomes an ever-changing scrapbook open to everyone who enters the kitchen.

A favourite painting, *left*, warms the sleek surfaces of a kitchen. With the simple addition of two pears to the scale, a pleasing still-life is formed. Keep delicate artwork in a kitchen away from the sink and cooker, because moisture and grease may damage artwork.

A magnetic board, *above*, offers a handsome alternative to covering a refrigerator with magnets. Here, it's mounted on a wall between cupboards and worktop, and holds recipes for the week's menu planning.

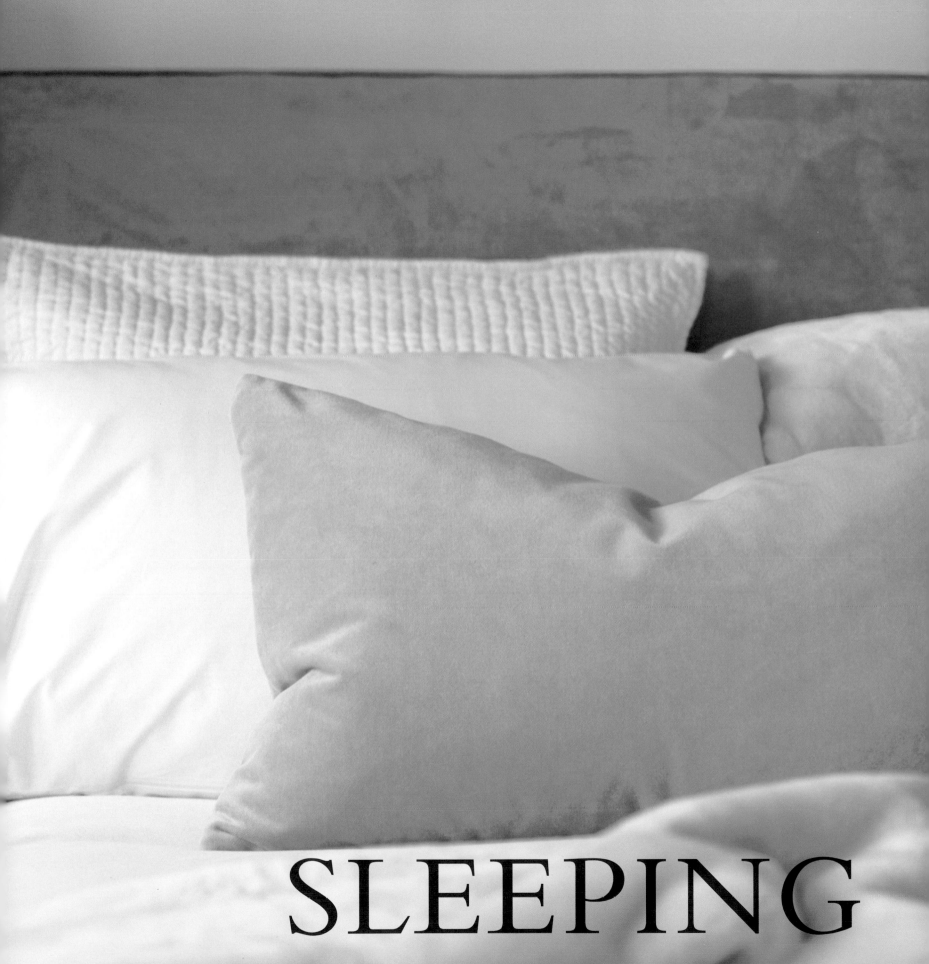

SLEEPING

"MY BEDROOM IS A PRIVATE SPACE DESIGNED FOR PURE COMFORT. I NEED IT TO BE FILLED WITH INVITING MATERIALS, SOFT TEXTURES, AND FAVOURITE MEMENTOS."

ELEMENTS OF A SUCCESSFUL

BEDROOM

The more time we spend at home, the more important comfort and flexibility become in our rooms. In the bedroom, where we may not only sleep but also exercise, work, unwind with family, and watch television, this is truer than ever. Bedrooms today need to accommodate all these functions while preserving a sense of peace and privacy.

As bedrooms become more multi-functional, they also become more open to inspired arrangements and styling that's in keeping with the home's other spaces. A sleeping space can go beyond the traditional set-up of bed, chest of drawers, and two bedside tables arranged in a standard configuration. The rooms we show you in these pages offer some new ways to start thinking about your bedroom, to help you create a space that meets your needs for both function and comfort.

How to Plan a Bedroom

For some people, the bedroom is exclusively for resting. Others view it as a multi-use space. No matter how you see the room, the fact remains: we spend a third of our lives in bed. Invest in the best quality and comfort.

The placement of the bed is the first consideration in planning bedroom layout. Ideally a bed should be positioned with the headboard against the wall and 60 cm (24 in) of space on either side for access and ease of making the bed (30 cm/12 in can suffice at a pinch). In terms of style, see pages 180–81 for information about selecting a bed that best suits you.

Storage is the next concern. Organized storage in the bedroom remains high on the wish list for most people and can be achieved by using cupboards efficiently (see opposite page) and in conjunction with chests of drawers, wardrobes, chiffoniers, or under-bed storage. Most chests of drawers have a depth of 51–56 cm (20–22 in); allow 107–120 cm (42–48 in) of clear space in front to open doors and drawers (76 cm/30 in is the minimum in very tight spaces). Clothes cupboards such as wardrobes tend to have a greater variance in depth and require the same clearance in front.

Bedside tables are another necessity. There should be enough room for books and magazines, a lamp both for ambient lighting and to shed light on reading, and an alarm clock, a jug, or other amenities that you like to keep at hand. Furnishings intended for other rooms are also welcome in the bedroom: bring in a glass-front china cupboard to showcase collections, for instance, or a sideboard with shelves to hold reading materials.

A LIVE-WORK BEDROOM

This soothing space is a comfortable haven by day or night. Its thoughtful design allows a workspace to be incorporated while keeping the focus on the room's main function: relaxation.

■ A HANDSOME WORKSTATION set in front of a bank of windows lets the bed take centre stage and creates a separate work zone that feels separate and unobtrusive.

■ RECESSED BOOKSHELVES are streamlined and attractive, and make plenty of room for office books as well as for personal reading materials and favourite objects.

■ MULTIPLE LIGHTING SOURCES provide ample light for all tasks. Layered curtains allow sunshine to be let in and controlled during the day and can block out light completely in the evenings.

MASTER SUITE

Though a current trend is towards planning larger master bedrooms, even a modest-sized space can be fitted with the amenities of a grand suite. A separate dressing area consolidates clothing storage, freeing up space for a sitting area, a writing desk, a library, or even exercise equipment.

A pair of easy chairs and an ottoman create a quiet, comfortable reading spot adjacent to bookshelves built below a double window.

Ample space has been allowed for passage at the foot of the bed, even with a vanity table, desk, or media cupboard placed along the wall.

ENTRANCE

Swing-arm lamps are mounted on the wall, making room for other essentials on the bedside tables.

BATHROOM

Built-in chests of drawers within the enclosed dressing area maximize clothes storage.

A walk-in wardrobe is a great luxury that provides storage in an efficiently organized space.

PLANNING A WARDROBE

The key to keeping a wardrobe organized and efficient is planning separate sections for specific types of garments. The following guidelines indicate the right amount of space needed for each section.

Dresses and Coats
These should hang in their own section from a high mounted rod; arrange items from shortest to longest. Allow 2.5–8 cm (1–3 in) of rod space for each garment.

T-shirts
Casual shirts should be folded, stacked, and stored in drawers or on open shelves. Folded t-shirts and casual button-down shirts require a space that's at least 23 cm (9 in) wide.

Shoes
Footwear is best stored on slanted open shelves or in cubbyholes. Plan a depth of 30–36 cm (12–14 in) and a width of 18–20 cm (7–8 in) per pair of shoes (20–25 cm/8–10 in for men's).

Install all rods 30 cm (12 in) from the back of the wardrobe, to allow 5 cm (2 in) clearance for hangers.

High rods for dresses and coats should be at least 109 cm (43 in) from the floor; allow 152 cm (60 in) for formal dresses.

Lower rods should be at least 107 cm (12 in) from the floor; install upper rods at least 90 cm (36 in) above lower rods.

CUSTOMIZED WARDROBE

Wardrobes of all sizes benefit from customized organization that utilizes every inch of available space. Divide the wardrobe into separate sections for different types of clothing: double-hung wardrobe rods for shirts, skirts, and trousers; high rods for dresses and coats; open shelving for sweaters and accessories; and cubbyholes or slanted shelves for shoes.

A dresser unit holds underclothes, t-shirts, and socks, and functions as a vanity table.

A bedroom is much more than a place to sleep. It's a retreat, a place in which to leave behind the stresses of the day and regain serenity. To make your bedroom a haven that you look forward to returning to every evening, furnish it exclusively with the textures and colours that calm you. Perhaps you've experienced the sense of having found a perfect retreat at a spa or luxury hotel. Recall that space and its relaxing effects. Remember the sumptuous fabrics and bed coverings,

CREATING A
SANCTUARY

THE BEDROOM IS THE MOST

PERSONAL ROOM IN THE HOUSE.

LOOK FOR WAYS TO MAKE IT A

PLACE THAT YOU LONG TO RETURN

TO AT THE END OF THE DAY.

the fresh fragrances in the room, the calming colour palette, and the sunlight playing across the furnishings. These are all elements you can bring into your own home. Find bedding fabrics, throws, and soft cushions that you love to nestle into, and layer the bed with them. Bring bouquets of flowers into the room to add soothing scents. Choose window coverings that let in sunshine during the daytime, and light a fire or clusters of candles to add a warming glow at night. Surround yourself with family photos and favourite treasures. The right combination of simple elements transforms an ordinary bedroom into a personal sanctuary.

A Natural Light

To create a naturally refreshing space, take advantage of an abundance of windows and embrace sunlight's soothing warmth.

Often, the first impulse for window treatments in a bedroom is heavy curtains. But natural light is so elementally restorative and soothing that we may do better inviting it in than shutting it out. Waking to wisps of daylight filtering through a window is a much calmer way to start a day than being jarred by an alarm.

Covering windows in sheer curtains provides daytime privacy (hang blinds or a double rod to layer on opaque coverings for night-time) and allows in plenty of glare-free light. Choose a white or monochromatic palette and use a light touch with accents, and you'll have a naturally calm, refreshing room. Introduce lots of comforting textures for tactile pleasure and visual interest.

WHY THIS ROOM WORKS

Oversize windows and a creamy white palette make this bedroom a haven that revels in natural daylight. The unifying use of white, carried out through a sophisticated mix of layered textures, projects serenity.

■ SHEER WINDOW COVERINGS on the large windows diffuse daylight, provide some daytime privacy, and add romance to the atmosphere.

■ RICH TEXTURES are everywhere: hemstitch, matelassé, and faux-fur bedding, an abundance of pillows and throws, and a textured wool rug.

■ A GENEROUS MIRROR placed opposite the window reflects daylight throughout the room.

■ A RAISED HEARTH gives the fireplace more focus and makes it visible even when lying in bed.

■ EASY CHAIRS, an ottoman, and a side table make the fireside an inviting spot for reading.

WHY THIS ROOM WORKS

Clean surfaces and a calming natural colour palette give this bedroom the feel of a meditative retreat. Plush yet simple furnishings add a welcome layer of luxury.

■ NEUTRAL TONES in the bedding, upholstered furniture, and woven rug and baskets extend a restful palette that begins with calming green walls.

■ LINEN PANELS are hung over bookshelves to give them a streamlined look and minimize visual clutter.

■ ROWS OF BASKETS tucked into the bed platform contain and conceal clothing and necessities.

■ GENEROUS CHAISE LONGUES face towards the window views, creating an area for quiet relaxation.

CREATING A SANCTUARY

Room for Reflection

A subdued palette and clever storage work together to eliminate distractions, making this bedroom a space for quiet contemplation.

Muted tones of colours found in nature are ideal for a bedroom: the browns and greys of tree bark and weathered wood, the rich creams of sand and stone, the fresh greens of spring and summer, and the cool blues of water and sky. Quiet natural colours, paired with uncluttered surfaces and smooth, cool-to-the-touch fabrics, create a contemplative, restful space.

Bring in furniture and accessories that extend the muted palette and are soft by design – chaise longues, chenille throws, an upholstered headboard, or an upholstered cube used as a bedside table. Reinforce the calming effect by minimizing visual clutter; you can even drape shelves with linen panels to conceal their contents. Find storage systems that are both visually appealing and useful. Baskets fit in all kinds of nooks and crannies, and they add pleasing texture. If you have a fireplace or a view, orient the furniture towards it to take advantage of a natural focal point for meditation.

Colourfully Calm

Borrow aspects of Eastern interiors to transform your bedroom into a colourful yet peaceful space for rest and reflection.

The art of repose is one that has been perfected by Eastern cultures. Integrating Asian design elements into your space – bamboo, silks, tapestries, and rugs – can conjure a sense of calm even in a vividly coloured room. Though subdued colours are most often thought of as calming, bright colours can also be used to evoke a restful atmosphere that's accented with exotic flair.

The use of screens, both as dividers and as decorative elements, is also an Asian tradition that translates well to a bedroom sanctuary. To subtly divide spaces in your room while adding a sense of romance, use carved or papered screens, or hang sheer panels of fabric from the ceiling to define areas and diffuse light.

WHY THIS ROOM WORKS

Vibrant colours and see-through fabric scrims create a restful atmosphere that evokes the romance of a Far East journey.

◼ **VOILE PANELS** hung from the ceiling delicately describe a "pavilion" around the bed. Attached with Velcro to bookcases, they also soften the strong lines and create a sense of unity throughout the room.

◼ **A PLATFORM-STYLE BED** reinforces the Asian theme and preserves a sense of openness in the space.

◼ **CRISP WHITE SHEETS**, a pale pink duvet, and silk shibori pillows cool down the hot colours.

◼ **INTRICATE MOTIFS** and well-chosen accents – kilim rugs, embroidered linen, and an Asian-inspired teapot – lend exotic touches.

◼ **OVERSCALE GLASS DOORS** open the room up to the back garden. The scrim fabric's translucence ensures that light and views are not obscured.

Bed Options

Today's beds are more luxurious and comfortable than ever, with an ever-widening range of sizes, materials, and styles to choose from. Given the amount of time that we spend in bed, choosing the right one is among the most significant furnishing decisions you'll make when decorating a bedroom.

Keep in mind that a bed's frame is larger than the mattress it holds, so take this into account when you're selecting a bed. Choose a frame with a sturdy headboard that offers solid support for reading. If you have lots of room, choose a frame that also has a footboard, for a finished look. If space is tight, opt for a frame with a slim headboard and no footboard. Platform beds forgo both head- and footboards, providing a completely pared-down look. Whatever style you choose, allow adequate space around the sides and end for traffic flow. A clearance of 60–90 cm (24–36 in) lets you manoeuvre most comfortably.

A platform bed, *right*, is a wonderfully versatile style, since it has no head- or footboard and can be positioned anywhere in a room. Here it's pushed against the wall and piled with pillows, giving it the look of an attractive day-bed that invites reading or lounging.

DESIGN LESSON CARING FOR BED LINEN

From a basic set of sheets to decorative duvet covers and pillowcases, bed linen provides a relatively inexpensive and easy way to refresh a bedroom. Good-quality cotton sheets start at 200 threads per 2.5 cm (1 in); the higher the thread count, the finer the quality of the sheet. The softness and lustre of cotton sheets are generally enhanced with each washing. You can lengthen the life of your bed linen by paying attention to the way they're cleaned and stored.

To store sheets, blankets, and pillows, choose a space with good air circulation. Keep fibres fresh and dry by placing linen in unlined wardrobes or drawers, unstained open-weave baskets, or acid-free cardboard boxes with loose-fitting lids.

■ WASH SHEETS ALONE, not with towels or other rough materials that can weaken the fabric's fibres.

■ USE COOL WATER and the gentle cycle on the washing machine to keep sheeting fibres strong. Select the extra rinse cycle if available; soap residue decreases the softness of linens.

■ SELECT COOL DRYER SETTINGS because heat weakens cotton fibres. Remove linen while slightly damp if you're going to iron them. Iron embroidered or lace pieces on the reverse side.

■ DRY-CLEAN COTTON BLANKETS that have a loose weave; washing them distorts the pattern.

■ PROTECT PILLOWS by encasing them in washable zippered protectors. Follow the care label for washing instructions, and use a low dryer setting to dry. Store unused pillows in a dry place.

Sleigh Bed

The graceful curves of the traditional wooden sleigh-style bed have endured over time. Today, sleigh beds are also available in iron, and some models have modified, open footboards. If you choose a classic wooden frame, head- and footboards are available in differing heights and styles.

Leather

Leather evokes the luxurious appeal of a cushiony armchair. In the bedroom, leather makes a bold statement that adds depth to the decor and brings immediate attention to the bed as a focal point. Tufted leather headboards, like the one shown here, create the ultimate comfort for reading in bed.

Iron or Brass Beds

Antique and reproduction iron or brass beds are an enduringly popular choice. An antique frame will require a new mattress that's up to date in comfort, and some may require a custom-size mattress to fit their smaller frames. New reproductions look every bit as appealing as originals, and are more readily available.

Wooden Panel

If you have limited space but still want the finished look and stability of a headboard, choose one with a very slim profile. You can make one from a panel of wood, attached either to the wall or the bed frame. Paint, stencil, or stain the wood any colour that co-ordinates with your space.

Natural Fibre

Wicker, cane, seagrass, and other natural fibres are striking choices for headboards. The simple silhouettes of natural-fibre bed frames bring casual, warm-weather style to a bedroom, and their textured open weaves have a lighter, airier effect than solid headboards.

Loose Covered

Swathing a headboard in fabric softens a bed and makes a more comfortable backrest for reading. Your choices are legion — go with stripes or solid linen for a tailored look, or floral cottons for romance. Loose-covered styles can camouflage existing headboards and can be removed for cleaning or refreshed with each season.

In the bedroom, where most of our personal belongings are stored, space is always a precious commodity. One of the most obvious ways to make the best use of space here is to eliminate clutter by keeping drawers and cupboards well organized. But there are many other ways to make a room more efficient. Take advantage of unused wall space and recessed nooks, especially under sloping or low ceilings where free-standing furniture may not fit. Tuck an inviting window seat, with storage

MAKING THE MOST OF
YOUR SPACE

WHETHER YOU HAVE A WEALTH OF SPACE FOR A BEDROOM OR VERY LITTLE, MAKE THE MOST OF IT. CREATIVE PLANNING HELPS A ROOM ACHIEVE ITS GREATEST POTENTIAL.

built into its base, into a sun-filled dormer. Fit other niches with customized shelving or built-in chests of drawers. Using every recess available in a space increases a room's functionality – and its character. Storage cupboards come in many sizes and styles and are hardworking and handsome additions to a bedroom. Choosing well-proportioned and appropriately scaled pieces also visually expands a space. In a small bedroom, furniture that is slim and scaled-down or high off the floor adds to an impression of greater space. In a bigger room, you have more of an opportunity to make a statement with large-scaled pieces.

Crisp fabrics and fresh accents bring new life to a master bedroom suite in a former attic. Positioning the bed in the dormer provides headroom and space for side tables.

■ A TRIANGULAR WINDOW creatively fitted into the side of the dormer makes the room seem more spacious and allows daylight to come flooding in.

■ SLIM FRENCH WINDOWS opening out onto a small balcony are custom-fitted to the peaked space, further extending the room's apparent size.

■ A PAINTED WARDROBE recedes visually as it is the same colour as the walls.

■ TWO EASY CHAIRS are loose covered in white to keep the look clean and airy. A voile cover on the round table gives it a light, ethereal quality.

MAKING THE MOST OF YOUR SPACE

An Attic Retreat

Privacy in a busy household is just a staircase away. Create a sunny and secluded bedroom suite in the found space of a converted attic.

The top storey of a hotel or a luxury apartment building is often considered the most desirable because of its privacy and prime views. When looking for space to locate a master bedroom, an attic is a wonderful option. By opening up your attic and filling it with light, you not only make the most of your home's space, but you also gain top-storey status for your private retreat.

The keys to a livable attic space are height and light. You need sufficient height to function comfortably, and as much daylight as possible to make the space energizing. Dormers are an invaluable addition because they increase both space and brightness. Windows and skylights brighten a room's interior and can make it appear larger than its actual dimensions. Look for any opportunity to add them, and consider non-standard locations and unusual shapes. Once you have the room's structure in place, sticking with a focussed colour palette keeps it looking simple, open, and spacious.

MAKING THE MOST OF YOUR SPACE

Wide-Open Space

If you've got a lot of space and want to celebrate it, remember: less is more. Keeping a large space simple emphasizes its openness.

Living in an open-plan room presents a different set of challenges regarding use of space. You may have so much of it that it's difficult to achieve separation between one area and the next. One option is to section off space with partial walls or large furniture pieces. Another is to use structural markers like columns or beams to subtly define boundaries and provide visual separation.

The great appeal of a space without divisions is its openness, so indulge in that sense of wide-open space. Choose sizable furniture pieces that suit the scale of the room and "float" them away from the walls for a serene effect. Add a few well-chosen accent pieces whose shapes complement the space. In an open-plan room, the sleeping area can often be seen from other areas, so it should look neat and be easy to maintain. Dressing the bed in neutral colours enhances the feeling of simplicity and calm, and lets you bring in bursts of colour through pillows and other accessories.

CREATIVE DISPLAYS AND CLEVER STORAGE FIND A HOME IN THE UNUSED SPACE AT THE FOOT OF YOUR BED.

A sideboard, *left*, typically used in a living room, is often the right length and height to fit neatly at the end of a bed. Here, the decorative red boxes and plaid fabric runner echo the bedding, so the piece appears perfectly suited for the room.

Wooden benches, *above and top middle*, offer space for holding small baskets and boxes on top and underneath, expanding the room's storage possibilities. Benches are also a place to drape extra blankets at bedside, and they provide a convenient seat for dressing. The light pine bench (above) holds accessories and serves as a dressing table — an especially welcome touch for guest bedrooms.

Two end tables, *top right*, can act as one long storage unit at the foot of the bed. A stack of books fills the space between, and a fabric runner draped across the top unites them. Baskets holding magazines slide under each table.

A folding table, *right*, offers a movable platform for bedside storage and display. In a guest bedroom, the table can be used as a luggage rack.

One of the greatest compliments a host can receive is hearing that overnight guests would like to return for another visit. That kind of encouragement makes having guests a great pleasure. Whether you're redoing a room or want to fit guest quarters into one that's used for another function, the first step is establishing a sense of privacy. Give visitors a space they can feel at home in. Make sure that even in a dual-use room, there's space for guests to unpack and claim an area as their own.

WELCOMING
HOUSE GUESTS

WHAT REALLY MATTERS TO GUESTS ARE SIMPLE PLEASURES. A PERFECT GUEST ROOM PROVIDES PRIVACY AND COMFORT, THEN ADDS TOUCHES THAT MAKE VISITORS FEEL SPECIAL.

Then, focus on the quality and comfort of the bed, choosing the best you're able to afford. Particularly if guests will be using a convertible sofa, test it yourself to ensure that the mattress is comfortable enough for a good night's sleep. Dress the bed in layers of fine fabrics that make guests feel pampered, and add small amenities to amplify a sense of welcome. A basket of muffins, a plush throw, a crystal pitcher of ice water, fresh new bars of special soap, and extra towels, blankets, and pillows – thoughtful accents are the mark of a gracious host. For a final touch, don't forget fresh flowers. Even one simple bud can soothe the senses.

An Open Invitation

Planning for guests' needs is the cornerstone of good hospitality. Create a space for visitors that you'd also enjoy escaping to yourself.

If you're fortunate enough to have space for dedicated guest quarters in a bonus room, studio, or cottage, you're in a perfect position for hosting visiting friends and family. Create a quiet hideaway that's ready to welcome visitors at a moment's notice by keeping it well-stocked and full of comforting amenities.

Approach the room's design as you might if it were a studio apartment. Think beyond a comfortable bed. Plan for places to eat breakfast, write a letter, or curl up with a book in the afternoon. Then fill the wardrobe with lots of blankets and bed linen, pillows, throws, towels, and bathrobes. Include an electric kettle and a basket of teas to make guests feel more at home.

WHY THIS ROOM WORKS

Set up to be both a getaway for the homeowners and a self-sufficient guest room, this airy space gives visitors the feeling of having their own private cottage.

■ A COMFORTABLE DAY-BED is a good choice for guest quarters since it doubles as a spot for relaxing, reading, or napping during the day.

■ A PEDESTAL TABLE presents a cosy spot for breakfast in the morning, provides a place to write a note or postcard at midday, and at night serves as a bedside table.

■ A WARDROBE offers generous storage for linen and bathrobes and leaves plenty of room for guests' clothing.

■ A STACK OF HAT BOXES doubles as a charming bedside table and can be pressed into service for storage.

■ BEAUTIFUL TEXTILES — cotton bedding, a matelassé quilt, a linen tablecloth, and a shag pile rug — provide pleasure and comfort.

The Gift of Serenity

An atmosphere of serenity is one of the most desirable assets a guest room can have. To create a calm retreat, furnish the space simply.

When travelling, sometimes the greatest luxury is a quiet place to rest. When planning a guest room, take a cue from gracious resorts and create a soothing, spa-like environment. Combine simple furnishings with high-quality luxurious fabrics and accessories inspired by nature to put a focus on reflective repose.

Start with the bedding. Rather than overdressing the bed, choose one or two covers in neutral colours that are crafted from invitingly tactile fabrics. Keep the room's furnishings spare and its colour palette soft, then add just one or two notes of stronger colour – perhaps an exotic flower or a decorative bottle of lotion – to gently punctuate the calm tone of the room.

WHY THIS ROOM WORKS

Guests find refuge in this bedroom's peaceful, cloistered quality. Furnishings are simple and serene, and accents have been chosen to reinforce the setting's air of calm.

■ A WALL-MOUNTED SHELF softened with a fabric runner holds bedside amenities, eliminating the need for a bedside table and giving the bedside area greater apparent space.

■ TEXTURED BEDDING and a hand-quilted coverlet bring focus to the comfort of the bed.

■ A RUSTIC WOODEN BENCH provides a simple spot to sit while dressing. Its unadorned style reinforces the pure simplicity of the decor.

■ A SINGLE BLOSSOM set in a bowl with floating candles further enhances the serene mood. Candles are used throughout the room to warm the space, and incense infuses the air.

■ A FEW UNDERSTATED ACCESSORIES give the room a finished look while maintaining its aesthetic.

Cottage Comfort

Offer guests a welcome change from the workaday world with a room that recaptures the simple charms of a summer cottage.

Think of a favourite lakeside cottage or beach house you enjoyed staying in long ago. Its pleasures were probably not about luxury but rather were related to cool breezes and catnaps on a rumpled bed, fragrant with the fresh scents of the outdoors. When you have guests coming to stay, help them cast off their cares by inviting them into a room that renounces any notions of fussiness and re-creates those feelings of easy comfort.

To import the unembellished cheer of a summer room into your space, start with a clean slate. An all-white background not only evokes the look of warm-weather whitewashing, but it also affords the greatest ability to change its appearance with a quick switch of bedding or accents. For furnishings, stick with the basics. A room free of clutter is many people's idea of heaven, so a comfortable bed, a modest bedside table, and a suitable lamp are the only essentials. Crisp bedding in bright colours adds instant appeal and completes the theme.

WHY THIS ROOM WORKS

Bright sunshine, whitewashed walls, and crisp bed linen are all that's needed to provide pleasure in this cheerful room whose picturesque charms recall summers at the lake.

■ **WHITE WALLS AND FLOORS** create a clean, refreshing background that reflects natural light and makes the room feel more spacious.

■ **PATTERNED FABRICS** like the gingham-checked sheets, matelassé quilt, and jacquard throw add inviting visual texture. Physical and visual textures are both especially important in a room that uses a lot of white, since texture more than colour supplies visual interest.

■ **A HEMSTITCH BED VALANCE** recalls a time when heirloom linen was reserved for special guests.

■ **PAINTED PANELLING WALLS** evoke the look and feel of a holiday home's sleeping veranda.

■ **ACCENT PIECES** are kept to a minimum and stay within the red-and-white colour scheme.

BATHING

"TO ME, THE BATH IS

THE ULTIMATE RETREAT.

IT SHOULD BE PRIVATE AND

SOOTHING, FILLED WITH

REFRESHING AMENITIES

AND PLEASURES THAT

ENGAGE ALL OF MY SENSES."

ELEMENTS OF A SUCCESSFUL
BATHROOM

More than ever before, a bathroom's decor can reflect the style and comfort of the rest of your home. Bathrooms were once hardworking no-frills zones – attractive, but functional first and foremost. Now, functionality remains important, of course. But the way we think about the bathroom has changed tremendously, and so much more is possible. A growing desire for balance in our lives means that the bathroom has become a larger part of our floor plans. It's a room to spend time in – a space not only for cleansing but also for rest and contemplation. The rooms in the following pages show just a sampling of what's possible when creating a bathroom that's filled with light, warmth, and comfort.

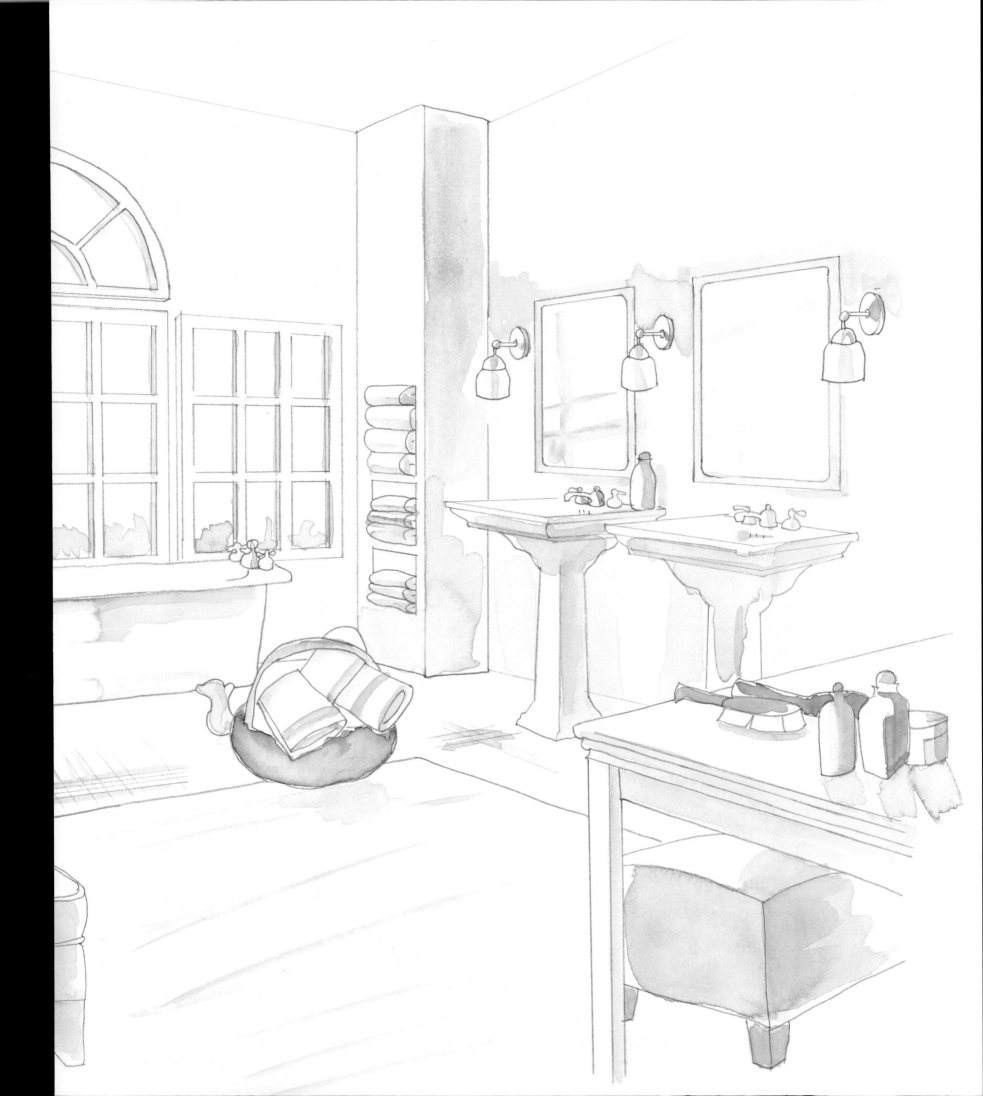

How to Plan a Bathroom

When planning an up-to-date bathroom for your home, take the space you have to work with and see how you can accommodate your decorating preferences. With so many options, a wish list is a good place to start.

In the bathroom perhaps more than in any other room, the best arrangement can be determined by noticing how you use the space. A lot can be learned about making your bathroom more functional and comfortable, even if you're not building a new one from scratch, and many furnishings or fittings can be added without major remodelling. For at least a week, pay attention to how you use your existing bathroom. Make a list of the things you'd do differently if you could. Do you see the bathroom as the one place you can escape to for time alone, or do you enjoy sharing it with the whole family? If you like lingering here and you're able to splurge on new fixtures, a soaking bathtub offers the ultimate spa-like escape, and a double-size cubicle with tempered glass walls makes showering a whole new experience. But for a similar effect without a large bill, simply bring in a comfortable chair, fit a steam shower or a deluge showerhead, or install custom lighting for reading in the bathtub. Similarly, look at your other needs and desires – for storage, lighting, and decoration – and realize that your options range from rebuilding to simply replacing the towels and shower curtain. Even small changes here can have a big impact. Compile your wish list based on thoughtful evaluation of day-to-day use, then enjoy exploring the decorating possibilities.

THE ULTIMATE BATHROOM

This sizable bathroom (above and preceding page) typifies a new approach to bathroom design. Used for rejuvenation as well as bathing, it incorporates furnishings from other rooms in the house.

■ A FREE-STANDING BATHTUB is an increasingly popular choice in today's bathrooms. This installation highlights the bathtub's sculptural shape.

■ GRAND WINDOWS, such as those you might find in a living room, wash the room in natural sunlight.

■ A WOODEN VANITY TABLE introduces natural texture and warmth to the room, offsetting the cool white surfaces. Baskets and plants add further texural interest.

■ A CHAISE LONGUE provides a cosy spot to linger and enjoy the sun and solitude.

BEDROOM

CLASSICAL SYMMETRY

A pair of console sinks shapes this straightforward plan for a bathroom that appears larger than its compact footprint would suggest. The floor plan gains symmetry from the two sinks flanking the cupboard and the toilet and shower flanking the bathtub.

Frosted glass walls frame the bathtub.

A free-standing cupboard stores toiletries within reach of both sinks.

Large mirrors behind the sinks visually expand the space.

The tiled shower cubicle includes a built-in bench, useful for shaving legs.

MASTER PLAN

A luxurious oval bathtub, set into a bay surrounded by windows, is the key feature of this master bathroom. Bottom-up window blinds screen the bather while letting in light and outdoor views at the top of the window.

A double-ended bathtub allows two people to soak. This one is encased in a large deck that offers room for towels and toiletries.

A heated towel rack is a little luxury that takes up very little space.

The worktop is lower in the centre; 71 cm (28 in) is a more comfortable height for a vanity unit than standard 90 cm (36 in) worktops.

BEDROOM

A floor-to-ceiling cupboard supplements under-sink storage.

A privacy door on the toilet enables the bathroom to be used by more than one person at a time.

The spacious shower has two showerheads.

SPACE REQUIREMENTS

Drawing a scale floor plan of your space will indicate how fixtures will fit into your room. You can try several different layouts until you arrive at one that best satisfies your needs. Work with the minimum dimensions below to allow ample room to move around.

30 cm (12 in)

60–90 cm (24–36 in)

Bathtub

Allow at least 30 cm (12 in) between bathtub and an adjacent fixture, 60–90 cm (24–36 in) between bathtub and a wall. A shower cubicle requires at least a 90 cm (36 in) square space; also, allow room for the shower door to open fully.

76–90 cm (30–36 in)

1.3 m (4.5 ft)

Toilet

A space of 1.3 m (4.5 ft) from the wall it is mounted on is needed for a toilet. Allow a width of 76–90 cm (30–36 in).

1.8 m (6 ft)

71 cm (28 in)

45 cm (18 in)

Sinks

A minimum of 1.8 m (6 ft) of worktop space is needed for two sinks. The centre of a sink should be at least 45 cm (18 in) from an adjoining wall. Allow a minimum of 71 cm (28 in) clearance to stand and use the sink.

This light-filled bathroom makes room for both functional pieces and decorative furnishings in its open, generous floor plan.

■ A WOODEN SIDEBOARD fitted with a marble worktop is typical of a new trend in bathrooms. A creative use of furniture in the bathroom adds interest and individuality to the space.

■ A CLAW-FOOT BATHTUB soaks up the sun in the bay window, creating a dramatic focal point.

■ SEAMLESS GLASS on a double shower adds to the sense of the room's expansiveness.

■ AN ANTIQUE WOODEN BENCH and a zinc table help keep the room personal and warm, balancing the space's grand proportions.

UPDATING THE CLASSIC BATHROOM

A Spacious Plan

Free the bathroom from its traditional box by creating a light-filled room rich with architectural details and unique furnishings.

The trend of allotting more space for a bathroom is indicative of a growing recognition of the room's importance in our lives as a space for rejuvenation. If you're fortunate enough to have a spacious bathroom, take advantage of its assets by flooding it with natural light and keeping it open and airy. In a room like this, a free-standing bathtub becomes a natural focal point, and positioning it near a window makes the most of the influx of light. Large windows, skylights, and even patio doors that open out into a garden are becoming increasingly common in today's bathrooms.

Shower stalls also have become larger and more luxurious. To make the most of a roomy shower, use seamless glass walls instead of a curtain, which creates a sense of spaciousness even in a small room. Take advantage of the wide variety of fittings and config-urations now available on the market, including "rain" showerheads, steam showers, and dual showers.

The Wet Room

Break the boundaries of the usual bathroom.
Dispense with dividers and design an open
space that celebrates the joys of bathing.

In a true "wet room", all surfaces are waterproof and
the space has a central floor drain, eliminating the need
for an enclosed shower cubicle. Less structured and
more freewheeling than a typical bathroom, wet rooms
let you luxuriate completely in the pleasures of water.

You might also choose to create a partial wet room,
waterproofing just the area within reach of the shower's
spray. Either way, the floor should be sloped to a central
drain to prevent water from pooling. Unpolished
materials such as slate make the best flooring choices,
as they offer more traction when wet than do smooth
surfaces. It's also wise to plan for a dry zone in the
room, so that towels and robes stay out of the spray.

WHY THIS ROOM WORKS

In this beautifully practical room,
surfaces are waterproof throughout
the space. An absence of dividers
or curtains lets water run freely
and makes bathing a joy.

■ LARGE WINDOWS let in air and
sunlight to help dry damp surfaces.
Textured acrylic window panels are
water-resistant and provide privacy.
Above the sink, where a mirror is
essential, windowpanes have cleverly
been fitted with reflective glass.

■ A FREE-STANDING BATHTUB rests on a
wide platform, which defines a shower
area in the corner. A floor-mounted
side tap allows bathers to rest their
heads comfortably at either end.

■ SLATE FLOORING is used throughout
the room for a natural look and for
enhanced traction underfoot.

■ STUCCO WALLS are treated with
water-resistant paint to protect them.

■ SMOOTH RIVER ROCKS and starfish
reinforce the water theme.

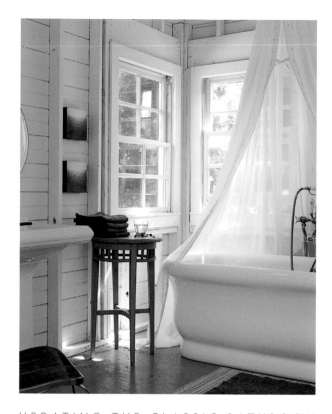

Furnishings typically found in other rooms are at home here, making this a dreamy place to refresh. Sited in a summer house, the room's exposed framework adds a cottage-like charm.

■ **WET AND DRY ZONES** are defined by smart furniture placement. Separation is further emphasized with rugs – terry cloth over crushed bamboo at the bathtub, deep pile in the seating area.

■ **A NET CANOPY** suggests romance and focusses attention on the striking free-standing bathtub.

■ **PLENTIFUL VENTILATION** helps this bathroom stay dry. Materials like cotton twill on the chair are bath-friendly, and the rustic wood surfaces are painted and sealed for protection.

UPDATING THE CLASSIC BATHROOM

A Furnished Bathroom

The new bathroom is more than a place for bathing. Furnish it with the comforts of a bedroom to create a space for relaxing.

When you have the luxury of space in a bathroom, transform the room into a private retreat by bringing in furniture, fabrics, and accessories that make you want to linger. Loose-covered furniture provides cosy spots for reading or unwinding (choose coverings in fabrics that are easy to change and wash such as twill, denim, chenille, terry cloth, or linen). Textured area rugs or patterned rugs like Orientals or kilims offer softness underfoot, and they also help delineate different areas. A chest of drawers meant for the bedroom can provide much-needed storage in a bathroom as well, where its wood tones warm up a room full of otherwise cool materials. When bringing wooden furniture into a bathroom, be sure it's painted or sealed to resist water.

In a furnished bathroom, it's important to create a floor plan that works well. A useful approach is to define zones for bathing, grooming, and lounging, allowing enough space so that non-bathing areas stay dry.

UPDATING THE CLASSIC BATHROOM

Material Choices

With so many options in materials, a bathroom can be tailored to any taste. Pair warm wood with cool metal and tile for a fresh, clean look.

Materials in the bathroom are by necessity chosen for functionality. With the array of choices currently available, there are also innumerable ways to showcase their beauty and combine them in surprising ways.

Tile has been used for centuries, but recent innovations in design and fabrication have made it more versatile than ever. Mosaic tiles, for example, are often used to give a bathroom a vintage look, especially tumbled stone or octagonal-shaped tiles. But when paired with up-to-date design elements – open wooden cupboards, stainless steel worktops, dramatic vessel sinks – mosaics look fashionably contemporary, particularly in newer styles like glass or metallic. Keep in mind that floor tiles in the bathroom must be slip-resistant, so some types won't be appropriate for bathroom flooring.

Sinks and Taps

Sinks are a major design element of the bathroom, and choices run the gamut from reproductions of classic styles to innovative new shapes. A sink may be a wall-mounted unit that takes up little space, or it can be set into the top of a cupboard that has storage space underneath. Vessel basins, mounted on top of a worktop, are a newer option. You can use almost any sort of vessel as a sink as long as it can be plumbed. Pedestal sinks are another option and also come in a wide range of styles.

Fittings, or trim – bath terms that apply to taps, handles, and other hardware – are as varied as sinks. Available materials include chrome, nickel, pewter, and stainless steel, all in polished, brushed, or matt finishes. Other options include the warm tones of brass, bronze, and copper. When choosing fittings, be sure the tap spout is long enough to flow directly over the drain. See Materials, page 358, for more about sinks.

A sampling of taps, *clockwise from top left,* shows the scope of styles available: a reproduction centre-set tap with lever handles; a classic English-style two-handle set with a teapot spout; a gooseneck tap; and a wall-mounted tap with single lever handle.

DESIGN LESSON LIGHTING THE FACE

When choosing lighting at the bathroom sink or mirror, the goal is to provide enough light so that you can see clearly when applying make-up or shaving. If using fluorescent bulbs, be sure to choose full-spectrum; normal fluorescents can give skin unnatural tones. Halogen bulbs also provide crisp white light. Whatever fixtures you choose, use translucent lenses or shades with them; clear shades can cause glare, and opaque ones block too much light.

Fixture Placement
To evenly light the face, a smart option is to mount fixtures at eye-level, approximately 168 cm (66 in) from the floor and about 76–102 cm (30–40 in) apart. Lighting from both sides is a smart choice because light from above may cast unflattering shadows.

76–102 cm (30–40 in)

168 cm (66 in)

Pedestal Sink

A classic bathroom fixture, a pedestal sink rests on a single column that partially conceals plumbing. Pedestal sinks give a bathroom a more spacious look because they take up less visual space than a vanity cupboard. Because pedestal styles don't offer the storage of vanity styles, be sure you have plenty of other storage options.

Wall-Mounted Sink

A smart choice for small bathrooms, a wall-mounted sink opens up floor space, creating the illusion of a larger room. The sink shown here is an updated interpretation. Its clever design encloses the plumbing and incorporates rails on which to hang hand towels. Look for a model with a wide deck around the bowl if you don't have a shelf or table nearby.

Vessel Sink

With the striking look of a decorative object, this new sink style harks back to the classic Victorian china washbasin that sat on every bedside table. Vessel sinks elevate the bowl to a height more comfortable for washing, and work best when paired with wall-mounted fittings. They are available in a wide range of shapes and materials, including glass, ceramic, and metal.

Corner Sink

This design is a great space saver, and, in some cases, the only style that will fit. Small corner sinks like this are a popular choice for powder rooms. Often, specialized sizes and shapes are available to solve awkward positioning problems. In this case, decorative moulding on the lower edge helps the sink blend in with the vintage-inspired bathtub.

Console Sink

Consoles have two or four legs and support a deck with one or two sinks. Two-legged models rely on the wall for some support. Originally made popular as reproductions of antiques, console sinks are now available in contemporary styles, too, and often incorporate towel rails into their design. Antique models can usually be found at architectural salvage outlets.

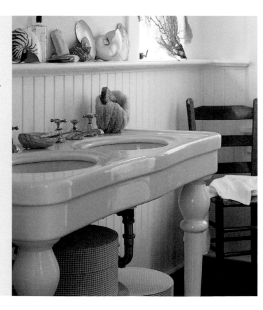

Washstand Sink

An antique washstand can be updated with modern plumbing to give period character to a bathroom. Here, a Victorian oak washstand with a marble slab deck and shelf was fitted to house two sinks. Wooden furniture adds warmth but should be sealed for water resistance. A chest of drawers can also be fitted with a sink, but plumbing will take up some drawer space.

In the past, when the entire family shared one bathroom, it was a challenge to schedule bathroom time. These days, many families have more space, but sharing is often still an issue. We all want a bathing area that's tailored to our needs. Mum may want things one way and Dad another; if children are sharing, they have their own special requirements, as do house guests. If it's not feasible to give each person a separate vanity unit and sink, there are still solutions for allowing everyone

ENJOYING
A SHARED BATHROOM

SHARING A BATHROOM IS A PLEASURE WHEN YOU'VE PLANNED FOR EVERYONE'S NEEDS. MAKE EACH FAMILY MEMBER AND GUEST FEEL COMFORTABLY CARED FOR.

a sense of personal space. Towel rails are easy to install, so assign one to each user – a great first step in making everyone feel cared for. Zone the room for maximum personalization and privacy, and plan storage that offers a place for everyone's individual items. Built-in cupboards are the most customizable and can range from a simple, cleverly divided undersink vanity unit to deluxe his-and-hers dressing areas; shelving is another flexible storage option that can be added to most rooms. Finally, make the bathroom both pleasant and practical by stocking lots of basic necessities like towels and tissue and finding attractive ways to display them.

ENJOYING A SHARED BATHROOM

Side-by-Side Style

Sharing a bathroom is sometimes a favoured choice. Couples can enjoy starting or ending a day together in a space that's built for comfort.

In busy households, the master bathroom is often a main communication centre where you assess the day's schedule or catch up at night after the kids are in bed. You need a bathroom that's bright and invigorating to start the day yet subdued and soothing at its end.

Equip the room to spend time in it. A music system, a small TV for the morning news, and an easy chair or chaise longue all help add to the comfort of a shared space. Keep candles, matches, and calming fragrances on hand so you'll be more likely to use them daily.

Nothing is better for energy than natural light, so uncover as many windows as possible and supplement daylight with lamps at the mirror, to evenly light the face for applying makeup or shaving. Flexible lighting can also deliver a more atmospheric effect at night. To subdue the lighting for evening, put overhead fixtures on a different switch from vanity unit lights, and use dimmers to give you greater control.

The Master Bathroom

Share your bathroom and enjoy the company. Make your master bathroom a stylish space that offers both togetherness and privacy.

If you share your bathroom with a mate but crave the comforts of a private domain, take the old his-and-hers concept to its new, luxurious conclusion. Create tailor-made spaces for each user that include not only individual sinks but also separate grooming areas, cupboards, and dressing areas. Allow space for storage of personal items near each sink or vanity, and keep shared supplies in a place convenient to both users. As in any room, a continuity of style is necessary for visual unity; look to the rest of your home for ideas and inspiration to make your bathroom into a retreat that's as stylish as any other room. Incorporating comfortable seating and fine materials like hardwood flooring and decorative panelling gives a bathroom unexpected sophistication.

WHY THIS ROOM WORKS

Designed for a couple, this generous master bathroom caters to each person's needs with separate his-and-hers areas for bathing, grooming, and dressing.

■ CUSTOMIZED ZONES are dedicated to each person – a vanity table for her, a chest of drawers for him.

■ A WINDOW SEAT offers a handy place to put on socks and shoes or a spot to rest after a hot bath.

■ A DEEP FREE-STANDING BATHTUB with a side-mounted tap is spacious enough for two to share comfortably.

■ NATURAL LIGHT, from a window over the vanity table, is ideal for applying make-up.

■ SOPHISTICATED MATERIALS, including decorative mouldings, dark wooden worktops, and hardwood floors, warm the room's white palette.

■ A PARTITIONED ALCOVE for the toilet provides privacy.

Every inch of space is maximized in this neat family bathroom. Good planning makes room for everyone's things, from toiletries and towels to kids' bath toys.

■ A DOUBLE-SIDED CUPBOARD divides the room for privacy and houses storage that's accessible from both sides. Shallow shelves for toiletries open to the sink side; deeper shelving for towels faces the bathtub.

■ PLASTIC BUCKETS are a practical and attractive storage solution for kids' bath necessities. A small stool helps youngsters get in and out of the bathtub and allows Mum to sit while young ones bathe.

■ A BUILT-IN LAUNDRY CHUTE is a smart detail that helps keep the space tidy and organized.

■ PERSONALIZED HOOKS make sure that everyone knows where to find his or her towel after bathing.

ENJOYING A SHARED BATHROOM

The Family Bathroom

Careful planning, creative furnishing, and plenty of storage contribute to making a family bathroom a pleasure to share.

A shared bathroom requires creative planning to comfortably accommodate the comings and goings of an entire family. The key is organization. One great option for storage is a unit that can double as a privacy screen or room divider. By making shelving accessible from two sides, you maximize its capacity. Each family member then has easy access to his or her own toiletries, and there's still plenty of room for basic bathroom necessities. If young children use the room, systems must be straightforward and easy to understand. Big buckets or bins and towel hooks with name tags let little ones know just where things should go. Empty walls, especially above the toilet, offer potential shelving space for additional storage, as does hallway space just outside the room, where additional cupboards may fit.

A bathroom that anticipates guests' needs gives them an inviting place to relax. Panelling on the walls and antique-style fittings give the room a period look.

■ **AN EN-SUITE SET-UP** is ideal for guest quarters, allowing visitors to have their own space filled with just-for-them amenities.

■ **BOUTIQUE-HOTEL TOUCHES** like fine toiletries and fresh bathrobes transform even a simple room.

■ **VINTAGE-STYLE CONTAINERS** hold decanted bath gel, shampoo, and conditioner; fresh hand-milled guest soaps add luxury.

■ **A STACK OF TOWELS**, a new pair of slippers, and some freshly cut greenery show the kind of personal attention that makes guests feel pampered.

■ **A NEUTRAL PALETTE** is a soothing backdrop that makes accents stand out and lets you adapt the room's look to the changing seasons.

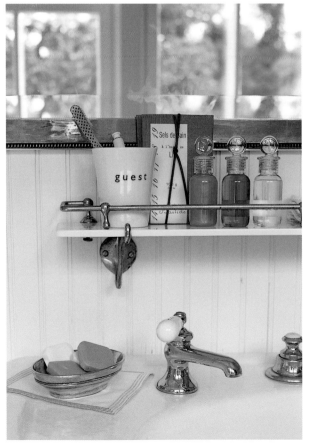

ENJOYING A SHARED BATHROOM

Guest Appearances

Small amenities and thoughtful details are an easy way to say "welcome" when preparing a guest bathroom for friends and relatives.

Sharing your home with house guests is a pleasure that's easy to enjoy when you've planned for it. Focussing on the details in a guest bathroom makes even a small space seem sumptuous. Stock the room with the kinds of amenities that you might find in a luxury hotel – toiletries like aromatherapy soaps, shampoos, and bath gel, and stacks of fluffy towels. Anticipate guests' needs by providing hard-to-pack items like a hairdryer and cosy bathrobes. Keep everything in plain sight so that guests are able to find things easily. Remember, too, that visitors will need space to put out their own belongings, so make room in the medicine cupboard and on worktops or shelves for them. Finally, add flowers or greenery to give the space fresh appeal.

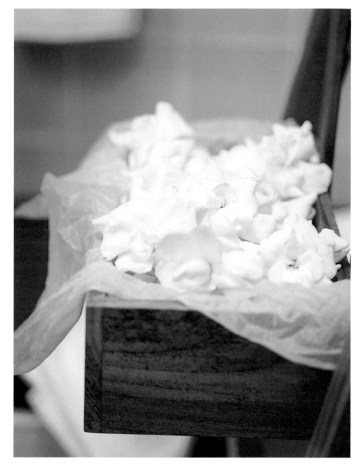

INDULGE YOUR GUESTS WITH THOUGHTFUL TOUCHES AND SIMPLE, LUXURIOUS AMENITIES THAT MAKE THEM FEEL WELL CARED FOR.

Handsome containers, *left*, a few well-selected toiletries, and a fresh orchid stem are the kinds of accent notes you'd find in a fine hotel. Amenities don't have to be lavish to make guests feel special.

Glass cake domes, *above*, showcase a tempting array of lotions, soaps, and colognes. An assortment of toiletries, presented creatively, gives guests the pleasure of sampling new products, which you can let them take home as gifts.

Gardenia blossoms, *above right*, in a wooden box lend their sweet scent to the bathroom; guests can toss flowers into their bathwater for a relaxing soak. Fresh flowers are one of the most appreciated accents in a guest room.

Men's grooming essentials, *right*, are arranged on vintage pewter trays. Trays are a convenient way to present guest amenities, because the entire collection can be easily moved or stored away.

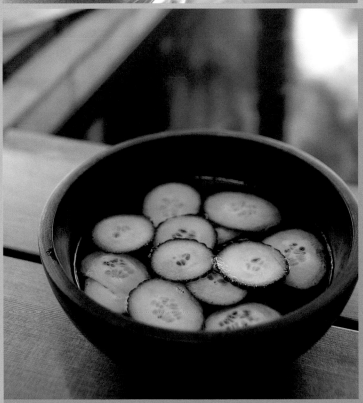

Few people have the pleasure of visiting a spa every day, but you can come close in your own home bathroom. Historically, a visit to a spa was known as "taking the waters", and water is still key to a spa experience, from mineral baths to Vichy showers. At home, deluxe fixtures like soaking bathtubs, which allow bathing immersed up to your chin, offer a spa-like indulgence in water. Most spa treatments end with a quiet rest, so a cosy chair or chaise longue is an especially sumptuous addition to

REFRESHING
BODY AND SOUL

SPAS ARE DEDICATED TO REJUVENATING BODY AND SPIRIT. RECREATE A SPA EXPERIENCE AT HOME WITH A BATHROOM DESIGNED TO DELIGHT THE SENSES.

your own bathroom. If you have less room to work with, your resting spot might be as simple as a sauna-like bench softened with piles of cushions. What's most important is making your surroundings as tranquil and pleasing to the senses as possible. Aim for a purity of space and furnishing that promotes serenity. Open the room to sunlight and views to the outdoors. Choose a restful colour palette, perhaps taking inspiration from water or nature. Enjoy the benefits of aromatherapy with bath infusions, fresh flowers, or candles, and keep stacks of luxury towels at hand. Stock soothing lotions and other amenities that make you feel pampered.

An At-Home Spa

Treat yourself to the ultimate bath experience. Incorporating a deep soaking bathtub into your bathroom turns it into your own spa.

In Japan, bathing is not something one does just to cleanse the body. It is a centuries-old ritual used to rejuvenate both body and spirit. A deep bathtub, called an *ofuro*, is filled with steaming hot water for soaking; cleansing takes place separately, prior to entering the ofuro. Many people spend at least half an hour each evening soaking in a bath, contemplating the day.

Fortunately, you don't need to go to Japan to relax. Soaking baths are now widely available for home baths (see pages 237 and 361). Custom-built baths can be made in any size, usually from cedar, redwood, or teak. Ready-made models, both free-standing and drop-in, are available in acrylic, fibreglass, metal, and wood.

WHY THIS ROOM WORKS

As aesthetically pleasing as it is physically comforting, this serene home spa with its traditional Japanese soaking bathtub soothes the senses in every way.

■ A CEDAR SOAKING BATHTUB filled with steaming water is roomy enough for several people to share. The platform is a traditional Japanese design and offers the warmth of natural wood.

■ CANDLES AND INCENSE scent the room. Soothing herbal bath infusions and aromatherapy oils are also at hand to enhance comfort.

■ A BUILT-IN BENCH and plenty of cushions provide a space for lounging, chatting, or meditating. A chaise longue offers a comfortable spot to stretch out before or after soaking.

■ NATURAL MATERIALS used throughout the room are practical, pleasing, and bath-friendly.

■ WALLS OF WINDOWS make nature an integral part of the setting.

Natural Senses

Bring the serenity of a spa to your bathroom with simple, sculptural shapes and a pleasing organic palette of colours and materials.

One way to bring spa style to a bathroom is by using an economy of ornament and opting for an elemental aesthetic. Choose simple fixtures and fittings, and pair them with colours, materials, and accents drawn from nature, to give a bathroom the feel of a luxurious retreat.

As with any furnishings in your home, simple pieces focus on purity of shape and contribute to a sense of spaciousness. Wall-mounted sinks leave floor space open below them; flush-mounted cupboards keep the wall plane unbroken; free-standing bathtubs' forms may appear less massive than built-ins. Complement this streamlined approach with natural materials like terra-cotta or stone, and bring in fresh greenery for accents.

WHY THIS ROOM WORKS

This city sanctuary is made luxurious with spa-style simplicity. Muted earth tones are a calming backdrop for crisp white fixtures and fresh green accents.

■ AN ACRYLIC SOAKING BATHTUB in a striking contemporary shape serves as the centrepiece of the room.

■ SIMPLY DESIGNED FIXTURES and furnishings — wall-mounted sinks, flush-mounted wall cupboards, a unique sculptural toilet — establish the room's quiet aesthetic.

■ SALTILLO FLOOR TILES are a sensual treat for feet and lend an earthy character to the room, grounding the high-style fixtures.

■ GLASS MOSAIC TILES wrapping the walls and ceiling of the shower cubicle give it a luminous quality.

■ POTTED PLANTS thrive in the humid bath environment and contribute to the spa atmosphere. Scented blooming plants are especially soothing.

Hand-held Shower, *right*
Nostalgia for early-20th-century bath fittings has spawned reproductions with modern functionality. This period set combines a bath-filler tap, crossbar handles, and a handheld shower, as well as a conventional showerhead at the top of the exposed vertical pipe.

Floor-Mounted Fittings, *far right* Taps that are mounted on the floor and situated at the centre of the bathtub allow bathers to lean back in comfort at either end of the bathtub. With the increased popularity of double-ended bathtubs, this configuration is becoming more and more common.

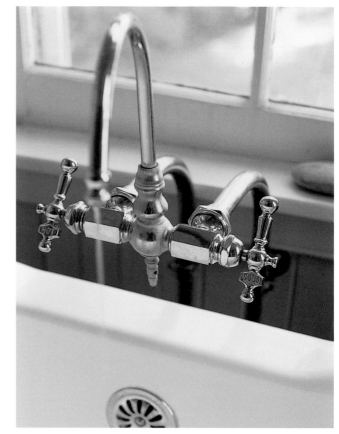

Deluge Showerhead, *right*
This circular showerhead style – also known as a rain or sunflower showerhead – simulates the feeling of an overhead downpour. Available in a variety of sizes, the sensation it delivers is an invigorating way to start the day. Bear in mind that these styles use more water than a conventional showerhead and so require a larger water-heater capacity.

Dual-Control Mixers, *far right* Shower mixers, like this classic Victorian design, have separate flow and temperature controls. Mixers in contemporary styles are also widely available.

Bathtubs and Fittings

When selecting a bathtub, size is a dual concern: a bathtub needs to fit the dimensions of your space, and it also must accommodate the dimensions of your body. Currently, standard-size bathtubs are 152 cm (60 in) long and 81 cm (32 in) wide, but you can find shorter models, or longer and deeper ones, in many styles.

While available floor space clearly plays a part in selecting a bathtub, your preferences for the type of installation and the look it gives the bathroom are also important. Free-standing bathtubs, such as the perennial favourite claw-foot, require a bit more space but offer flexibility because they can be positioned anywhere in the room. Built-in bathtubs are also classic, and they're increasingly being skirted in wood, tile, or stone to make them appear more like furniture. The fittings that you choose (see opposite) should complement your bathtub but don't have to be the exact same style. For more information on bathtubs, see Materials, page 361.

Bathtub styles, *clockwise from top left*: a classic roll-top bathtub with a wooden side panel and marble deck; an Empire-style free-standing bathtub with floor-mounted fittings; a whirlpool bathtub with concrete surround; and a reproduction claw-foot bathtub.

DESIGN LESSON ADDING A SOAKING BATHTUB

A luxurious new option in bathtub design has made its way from the spa into home bathrooms: the soaking bathtub. These bathtubs are several centimetres deeper than conventional ones, allowing you to fully immerse yourself for a more relaxing experience. Just as other bathtubs, they come in a variety of shapes, sizes, and materials, including enamelled cast iron acrylic, ceramic, copper, vinyl, and wood. The defining feature is depth. Most are 51–56 cm (20–22 in) deep, as compared to 36–41 cm (14–16 in) in a conventional bathtub. Some models, styled after Japanese ofuro soaking bathtubs (see page 232), allow you to sit upright in the water and can be as deep as 86 cm (34 in). Many designs also offer whirlpool options.

There are several factors to bear in mind if you're thinking of incorporating a soaking bathtub into your bathroom.

■ WATER CAPACITY It can take 227–284 l (60–75 gal) of water to fill a standard soaking bathtub (compared to about 159 l/42 gal for an ordinary standard bathtub), so make sure your water heater has the capacity to provide that much hot water efficiently.

■ WEIGHT Three hundred litres of water weighs about 303 kg (667 lb). The bathtub itself can run from 57 kg (125 lb) for acrylic to up to 227 kg (500 lb) for an enamelled cast-iron bathtub. Make sure your flooring structure can support the weight.

WORKIN

"MY HOME OFFICE NEEDS

TO BE CREATIVE AS

WELL AS FUNCTIONAL.

I WANT THIS SPACE TO BE

A SOURCE OF NEW IDEAS

AND FRESH INSPIRATION

FOR EVERY PROJECT."

HOME OFFICE

It used to be that "home" and "office" were concepts as separate and opposite as one could imagine, and we worked hard to keep things that way. Nowadays, the lines are less distinct, and many of us work at home at least part of the time. Make your home a place where you can get work done, and make your office a place that feels like home. Designing a workspace that's an integrated part of your house and in harmony with its decor is a win-win situation. A handsome home office encourages productivity while still offering home-style comfort. In this chapter, we've chosen a few of our favourite spaces to show you, to help you imagine what's possible in creating a great workspace.

How to Plan a Home Office

When planning the layout of your home office, learn from the concept of the kitchen work triangle, which allows for the most efficient use of space. An L-shaped, U-shaped, or galley arrangement puts everything within easy reach.

Wherever your office may be, you'll find work easier to organize if you have two principal work areas: one in front of the computer and another for doing phone- and paperwork. Plan, too, for easy access to file storage, your printer/fax/photocopier, and daily supplies. With a compact L- or U-shaped layout, you can pivot from one area to the other easily. The same is true for a galley set-up, where you sit between parallel work surfaces. The way you want your office to appear to visitors also influences decisions on its arrangement. For

instance, an L-shaped workstation may leave you and your paperwork on view to guests or clients, whereas a galley allows you to stow ongoing work in a cupboard that sits behind you. Store things that you use on a daily basis (phone, files, pens, clips, staplers, and so on) within arm's reach, no more than 90 cm (3 ft) away from the side of your chair. Less-used items and archival records are better stored outside your immediate work area.

Remember to include space for displaying things that are comforting and inspiring to you – not just family photographs but also art and decorative objects, perhaps related to your business or a hobby. An "inspiration board" can boost your creative energy; fill it with post-cards, magazine clippings, and work that you admire. Make sure you include an easy chair so you can review papers in comfort or simply relax and take a break.

AN ORDERLY L-SHAPED OFFICE

This office (above and preceding page) takes up little floor space and defines its work areas with linear storage. This compact set-up could fit onto a landing or in another small space.

■ A CONSISTENT STYLE of office furniture creates a sense of order, and individual units offer specialized storage. A corner desk area is included for computer work, and another desk bay is available for paperwork.

■ A BULLETIN-BOARD UNIT is a valuable information centre that holds a calendar, important notes, and inspirational images.

■ DAYLIGHT makes any workspace more pleasant, but windows can create glare, so position the computer monitor so that light strikes it from the side.

IN A GUEST BEDROOM

Because a guest room is used only occasionally, it makes good sense to take advantage of the space for use as an office. Plan concealed storage that allows you to quickly tidy up.

CUPBOARD

HALL

BATHROOM

A pair of attractive wooden filing cabinets are used as bedside tables – a clever way to introduce dual-use pieces into the room.

A cupboard or chest of drawers can be customized with special storage systems to keep business equipment and supplies out of sight. It also offers space for guests to store their belongings.

A wall of shelves provides generous storage for books and files. Use boxes and baskets to organize loose items among the shelves.

An upholstered chair is an asset in any office, providing a comfortable place to read and review work; it's also a nice amenity for guests.

Adjustable-arm work lights clip onto the shelves, providing accent lighting and visual warmth.

With no wall space to spare, a small desk fits neatly at the foot of the bed; an extension cord runs under the bed to power a desk lamp.

A DEDICATED WORKSPACE

An extra bedroom is well suited for conversion into a home office that uses a wall of cupboards as its primary storage space. Choose a desk and comfortable chairs from a home-furnishings shop rather than an office-supply shop, to better complement the rest of the home's interiors.

ENTRANCE

Opt for lateral filing cabinets, which are only 45 cm (18 in) deep and so fit easily into a standard cupboard.

A separate worktable has shelving built in below. It offers a place to keep files, papers, and other day-to-day necessities at hand.

Comfortable chairs are a must for clients and also allow you to take a break.

OFFICE COMFORT

You're more productive when you are at ease in your workspace, which means setting computer equipment at a comfortable height and providing sufficient lighting (lighting for desk work is addressed on page 351). Use this checklist to position your office furniture.

Forehead height, arms' length from face

74 cm (29 in)

69 cm (27 in) or elbow height

Computer Screen
Your monitor should be directly in front of you with the screen at arm's length and the top of the screen no higher than your forehead.

Keyboard
Though standard desk height is 74 cm (29 in), most people are more comfortable typing with their hands at about 69 cm (27 in). To determine the best height for you, sit in a desk chair with your arms bent at your sides; the keyboard should be at the height of your elbows.

Desk
A minimum space of 76 cm (30 in) square is needed for most desk work, adequate for a computer screen, phone, and letter-size papers. Allow at least 90 cm (3 ft) of clearance behind the desk for a chair.

Worktable
A small worktable on castors, about 66 cm (26 in) high, is a handy addition. Use it to hold files and supplies you'll need for the day, or use it as your computer station to keep your main desk clear.

Once you've decided to claim a space for an office in your home, you need to make it workable. More to the point, you need to make it work *for you*. What does your ideal workspace look like? There are basic elements that apply to almost any room, of course, like smart space planning, sufficient lighting, and adequate storage. But which choices can you make to create an office that is inspirational as well as functional? First, find the right space in your home, whether an attic retreat or a corner

DESIGNING A
HOME OFFICE

TO CREATE AN IDEAL WORKSPACE, TRUST YOUR INTUITION. FIND THE COLOURS, FURNISHINGS, AND TYPES OF SPACES THAT PLEASE YOU, AND LET THEM GUIDE YOUR DESIGN.

of the kitchen. Then, make sure it's efficiently planned and comfortably furnished. Think about whether you prefer traditional furniture or creative alternatives: a classic desk, or a sheet of wood set across filing cabinets? Pay attention to which colours you respond to, how much light you like, and which little extras give you a sense of luxury, and let these details inform your design choices. Storage figures prominently here, and one of the keys to a smart-looking office space is keeping it clutter-free. Remember that you're at home, though: think beyond the filing cabinet, and find imaginative or whimsical alternatives to standard office pieces.

DESIGNING A HOME OFFICE

An Attic Office

If you need space for an office, a roomy attic is a top-flight option. Create an airy workspace that's high above the bustle of home.

An underused attic may prove to be a hidden treasure when you're looking for office space. Attics often have plenty of space that you can put into service, and they offer a romantic sense of being in a creative hideout.

If your attic is currently an unfinished space, several key issues should be addressed before transforming it into a work area. You'll need to make sure that ceiling height and floor support are sufficient, and that your electrical capacity can handle the day-to-day demands. Consult a licensed professional, too, about insulation and venting, as attic temperatures can affect your comfort as well as your office equipment's ability to function.

Once you get the go-ahead, remember that in a small enclosed room, less is more. Bathing the space in light (skylights are ideal) and using a neutral colour palette enhances an attic's airiness. Bringing in lightweight, small-scaled furnishings that best fit under the eaves also keeps it looking streamlined.

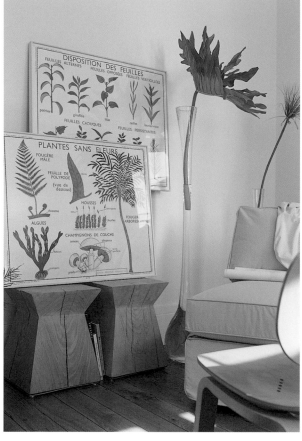

Signature Style

Any room benefits from a creative approach to design. A home office is especially distinctive if it reflects your work's character.

Resourceful ideas are the foundation of one-of-a-kind style. Even if you're designing on a budget, there are plenty of ways to give any room a signature style if you adopt an inventive approach to furnishing.

Office furniture can be assembled from the most basic components. While shop-bought modular pieces offer great flexibility, try inventing your own: create a desk by placing a sheet of wood over two filing cabinets or saw-horses; fashion a shelving unit from boards and storage cubes or planks and a stepladder. For inspiration, look to the work that you do. Gear decorative displays to a work theme, and make a virtue of necessity by showing off the tools of your trade and fruits of your labour.

WHY THIS ROOM WORKS

A landscape designer grows a business in this serene, garden-like setting with its fresh colour palette, inventive furnishings, and work-related decorative displays.

■ A SAWHORSE-BASE DESK topped with wood blends with the natural surroundings and is a low-cost way to create a large work surface.

■ SIMPLE WOODEN SHELVING UNITS are sturdy yet inexpensive.

■ A SOFT, BRIGHT WALL COLOUR is an ideal backdrop for exotic plants and botanical artwork.

■ CLIENT PRESENTATIONS and work books contribute to the decor.

■ MODULAR WOODEN STOOLS are reminiscent of tree trunks and bring the spirit of the outdoors inside.

■ ARMLESS UPHOLSTERED CHAIRS are easily rearranged to create a comfortable conference area.

■ WINDOW SHUTTERS block glare and offer privacy but let in sunlight.

A Meeting Place

Part of good design is creating a space that suits all of its users. A polished workplace is a pleasure for you and your clients alike.

Inviting clients and associates into your office is one of the joys of working from home. You get the pleasure of welcoming guests into your personal space in a way that's just not possible in a corporate setting. To impart a professional impression, make sure the room offers the comforts of home but has a businesslike demeanor. This doesn't mean standard office furniture is required. Any furnishings that are clean-lined but comfortable can project an at-work ethic. Choose rugs, coffee tables, floor lamps, and accessories that add a casual sense of ease. Display colourful aspects of your character in the room to add personality and warmth. A bulletin-board collage or a favourite collection on the bookshelves gives visitors a peek into your personal life.

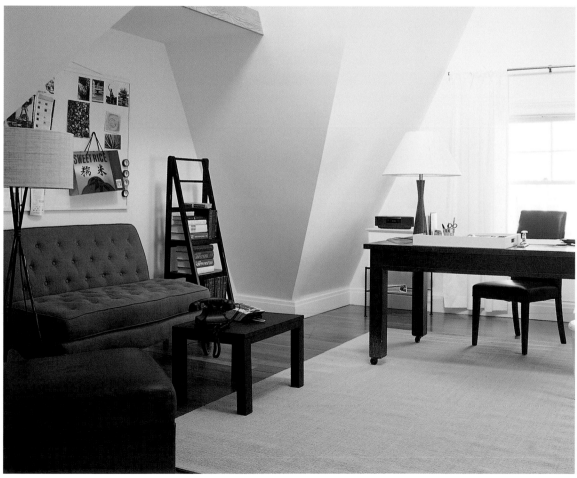

WHY THIS ROOM WORKS

This light-filled attic room uses no traditional office furniture yet it has a professional feel. An eclectic blend of furnishings works together to create a home-like setting for business.

■ A MIX OF FURNITURE STYLES creates a more personal mood than a suite of matching office furniture: a contemporary chair is paired with mid-century lamps and a retooled vintage love seat.

■ THE MOBILE DESK is an oak library table set on castors. It's positioned by the window to take advantage of natural light, but it can be moved against the wall to make space for larger meetings.

■ AN OVERHEAD SHELF, built between the eaves, holds flat files out of the sightlines of visitors.

■ A BLACKBOARD TABLE adds a touch of whimsy and lets callers jot down notes and numbers while using the phone.

■ THE SIMPLE PALETTE of white walls with brown and black furnishings projects a handsome, professional air.

With so many hours of our lives spent working, it's well worth the time and effort to create a workspace that is as beautiful as it is functional. And since it's an integral part of your home, there's every reason to make it as inviting and well-planned as your living room or bedroom. When determining the decor of your home office, look to your other rooms for clues on colour and style. Especially if your office is within the traffic flow of the rest of the house, you'll need it to blend in with

WORKING IN STYLE

A HOME OFFICE IS AT ITS BEST WHEN IT LETS YOUR PERSONALITY SHINE THROUGH. CREATE AN ENVIRONMENT THAT STIMULATES AND INSPIRES YOU TO DO YOUR BEST WORK.

the surroundings, so design it with a colour palette, furnishings, and accessories that are consistent with the style of adjoining rooms. If your office shares a room used for other purposes, a cohesive style is even more important. All that said, if you're fortunate enough to have a separate space, indulge in a little luxury. You've made it to your own executive suite, so invest in well-crafted furnishings and fine finishes, and treat yourself to a terrific desk lamp or accent piece that you'll love looking at. Likewise, be imaginative with displays. You're free to reveal more of yourself than the standard family photo, so bring in artwork and personal collections.

In Good Working Order

An office that's open to view demands a clear sense of order to maintain its style. Keep projects contained in neat walls of storage.

Order helps establish a sense of calm, and that becomes increasingly important when your home office is also used by the family for other purposes. Put miscellany in its place and you'll have a harmonious haven for all of a workroom's different functions.

One of the best ways to contain office hodgepodge is to take advantage of wall space. The smartest options for a neat look include modular storage and bookshelf arrangements. Shelving is extremely versatile and makes room for everything from reference books and neatly arranged baskets of paperwork to favourite objects or collections. Cupboards or bins with doors or lids conceal the odds and ends that might otherwise disorder a work surface. If you paint shelving or storage units the same colour as the walls, the units will be less obtrusive and will have a built-in appearance.

WHY THIS ROOM WORKS

With an abundance of desk space and modular wall storage, this office also functions as a family study and den. The symmetrical bookshelves and distinctively arranged cube cupboards bring orderliness to the room.

■ **WALL-MOUNTED FILING CABINETS** provide concealed storage and, arranged in a random pattern, work as an artistic display.

■ **BUILT-IN BOOKSHELVES** contain reference materials for work and books for family reading, honouring both functions of the space.

■ **THE TOP LEVEL OF SHELVING** is kept clear of objects and clutter, preserving a sense of spaciousness that would be sacrificed if it were filled.

■ **A WHITE COLOUR SCHEME** creates an illusion of a larger room. The white work surface and storage units all appear to recede into the walls.

■ **A CONTEMPORARY SOFA** adds an energetic punch of colour. Its sleek style is perfectly suited to the room's sense of order and openness.

WORKING IN STYLE

An Office Landing

In an open space, creating a harmony of style between your office and the rest of the house is an essential part of successful planning.

When choosing a spot for an office, you may not have a room to spare, but you might still have room. Pick an area in your home where there's at least a partial wall that you can devote to a bookshelf, and enough floor space for a desk and chair, and create your office there. A generous stair landing, hallway, alcove, veranda, or bay window might suffice, with a little planning.

The most important aspect of making this work is creating a harmony of style. Furnish the office in ways that echo the surrounding or adjoining room's decor to maintain your home's cohesive look. For an in-the-open office, it's best to choose furnishings that occupy little visual space. Avoid heavy office furniture and opt instead for pieces with glass tops and slender profiles. Find ways, too, to ensure that you won't be disturbed during working hours. Creative design elements such as sliding doors, curtains, and screens close off space when necessary but maintain a sense of flow.

ADD STYLE AND WIT TO YOUR WORK SPACE WITH VINTAGE ACCESSORIES. CLEVERLY RE-PURPOSED TREASURES BRING ORDER TO POST AND PAPERS.

An antique hotel postbox, *opposite top*, is mounted on a wall and given new life as a bill sorter.

A metal letter "U", *opposite bottom*, part of an old shop sign, finds new purpose as a magnetic memo board. A combination of magnetized clips, pushpin-style magnets, and small dot magnets are used to make sure business cards, notes, and clippings are easy to find when you need them.

A gilded picture frame, *left*, with a glass inset, is put to work as a bulletin board. Notes and photos are taped to the surface, and a dry-erase marker writes easily on the glass.

Letter racks, *above*, can be custom-made or cannily reinvented. A pair of springs are stretched between two U-bolts (top); a vintage toast rack becomes an organizer for oversized envelopes (bottom).

Sometimes the only way to find space for a home office is to press another room into service and create a dual-purpose space. Kitchens, bedrooms, guest rooms, and family rooms all can be recruited to offer at least part-time office area without sacrificing their original functions or atmospheres. When considering candidates for an office spot, think about how the space is generally used. If a room tends to lie dormant during the daytime, you can probably claim at least one of its walls for a primary

WORKING
IN A SHARED SPACE

DIFFERENT ROOMS OFFER DIFFERENT ADVANTAGES FOR A WORKSPACE, BUT WITH CAREFUL PLANNING, YOU CAN CREATE A SEAMLESS BLEND OF HOME AND OFFICE IN ALMOST ANY ROOM.

workspace. Also, base your decision on the type and amount of work you do. Kitchens are better suited to lighter tasks like paying bills and making schedules; bedroom offices are well suited to reading and writing but less welcoming to office equipment or piles of paperwork. A family room or infrequently used guest room, where you can carve out a larger area, usually works best if you're setting up a full-time home office. Wherever you site it, design and style your office in ways that keep it comfortable and residential; look for furniture, light fixtures, and accents that harmonize the overall space and extend a sense of home.

WHY THIS ROOM WORKS

An all-white family room hosts a spacious office in a corner behind an ample sofa. The fabrics and colour scheme are the same throughout the space, making the work area a natural extension of the living area.

■ A BUILT-IN SOFA acts as a half-wall and a dividing partition. In this space-saving design, its frame incorporates a narrow work surface behind it.

■ OFFICE STORAGE is contained out of sight below the level of the sofa; open shelving puts some storage on display.

■ WALL-MOUNTED HALOGEN LIGHTS can be focussed upwards to fill the space with ambient lighting or downwards for task or accent lighting. Desk lamps spotlight specific desk areas and add to an at-work feel.

WORKING IN A SHARED SPACE

A Corner Office

Take advantage of today's sizable family rooms. There's plenty of space to set up for work while preserving an area to relax and play.

Many homes offer the comfort and spaciousness of a spare or family room. These are ideal places to section off a home office since they're often free for use during the day when kids are at school or out at play.

To ensure that family time doesn't distract from work hours – and vice versa – you'll need to define some boundaries around the office area. Furniture placement and lighting can help here. Position a large piece of furniture like a sofa, bookcase, or entertainment centre to form a "wall" behind which you'll work. In a casual family space like this, you don't want a complete barrier, just a subtle divider that delineates your work zone. You can use lighting to reinforce the line between living and work areas, too. Spotlights, wall fixtures, and desk or ceiling lights focussed on the workspace let you "turn off" work when it's time to focus on family and friends. As with any divided space, maintain a cohesive decor across both areas to keep it attractive.

A Bedroom Office

Bringing work into the bedroom can be a pleasure when your office space blends in serenely with the rest of the room.

It's challenging to bring a workspace into a room that's devoted to rest, but a thoughtful choice of furnishings can create harmony between sleeping and working areas. Planning a bedroom office carefully means you won't be interrupted by work when it's time to sleep, and the bed won't beckon when it's time to work.

Whatever your bedroom's decor, there's such a range of work surfaces and storage units available that you're bound to find one in a compatible style. You may also choose from a whole array of residential furniture that can effortlessly make a switch to office work, such as dining tables or sideboards and upholstered chairs.

There are other tricks to blending a workspace into a bedroom. Choosing dual-purpose furniture – using a small desk as a bedside table, for example – keeps a space subdued. Decorative storage pieces also preserve the sense of serenity by stylishly containing clutter.

WHY THIS ROOM WORKS

An entire workspace fits peacefully into an alcove of this bedroom. The architecture subtly defines the office, and the furnishings blend in effortlessly with the serene mood.

■ **RESIDENTIAL FURNISHINGS** at the desk – a table lamp and an upholstered chair on castors – fit well into a bedroom setting.

■ **A DINING-SIZE TABLE** suits the spacious bay and adds to the residential feel; its simple styling creates a tranquil, subdued effect.

■ **A WOODEN BENCH**, accessible from both areas, acts as an unobtrusive divider between work and sleep areas.

■ **STACKS OF BOOKS** topped by stones make attractive displays. They subtly reinforce the room's division.

Adds Up to a Championship Game

Feeling No Pressure,
The Illini Strike Again

RELAXING

"MY DREAM HOME INCLUDES PLACES FOR PURE RELAXATION. I WANT EVERY SPACE TO OFFER REASONS TO STOP AND LINGER, TO MAKE RELAXING IRRESISTIBLE."

LEISURE SPACE

Everyone needs time for relaxation, and if you make room
for it in your life, you're actually more likely to take the
opportunity to unwind. All throughout your home, indoors
and out, find ways to carve out spaces that are so soothing
and inviting that you simply have to slow down and settle in.

Leisure time means different things to different people and
embraces every kind of activity, both solitary and shared. So
make the TV viewing area, the patio, your crafts room, the
veranda, and the kids' playroom all as enticing as you would
your living room or bedroom. In the following pages, we'll
show you easy ways to do this, to bring style and comfort
to all the places where you and your family relax.

How to Plan a Leisure Space

The best way to manage stress is to build free time into your schedule because, left to chance, you almost never take it. A similar rule applies to your home. Create spaces devoted to leisure, and your family will use them.

Communal activities have different requirements from solitary pursuits, but both deserve priority when decorating your house. At home you have the best opportunity to encourage children's talents and interests. One way to do that is to make sure there's room to pursue them. Making space for creativity is one tangible way to stress its significance. Space to work on your own projects is equally important. Look for an underused room – or just a portion of a room or even a large cupboard – that will allow you to enjoy your

creative time without having to organize everything each time you want to work, whether on sewing or calligraphy, making a scrapbook or woodcarving.

Setting up a media centre is a popular way to bring the whole family together. Now sometimes built right into new homes, media centres are also easily added to spaces within your current home. Basements and unused attics are well suited to film watching because there are fewer windows to create glare on the screen. If you have a spare bedroom, that's another ideal location because it's possible to darken the space with black-out blinds or curtains with black-out linings. Cupboards are ready-made storage areas for overflow CDs, the DVD player, the receiver, and the satellite box. On the opposite page, we've outlined a number of things to keep in mind to ensure your enjoyment of a media centre.

A COMPACT MEDIA ROOM

A media room (above and preceding page) occupies a wide landing at the top of the first-storey stairs. Windows were excluded from this area to prevent glare on the screen.

■ SECTIONAL SEATING suits film viewers of all ages. An ottoman on castors serves as a foot stool or coffee table, or provides additional seating.

■ BLACK CUPBOARDS are a good choice surrounding a video screen. It makes the TV less noticeable when it's off and minimizes the visibility of speakers in the unit.

■ PLENTIFUL STORAGE is critical to contain all the paraphernalia associated with TV, films, and music. Plan appropriately sized, built-in units to store similar items together, so that everything will be orderly.

CUPBOARD

Put your worktable in the centre of the space, when possible, so that you can walk around the work on all sides.

A large work surface can be inexpensively made from a sheet of plywood covered in replaceable self-sealing plastic, which is an ideal surface for cutting.

A SEWING/CRAFTS ROOM

For anyone who passionately pursues a hobby, setting up a dedicated studio or workroom at home can be a turning point in nurturing the creative process. Even a space of your own needs a logical layout, however, so tailor it for your particular craft.

A shelving unit provides vertical storage without taking up much floor space. Fill it with baskets that hold various materials.

Use filing cabinets, stacked drawer units, and other storage systems as supports for a desk or worktable to make the most of the available space.

ENTRY

CUPBOARD

FAMILY PLAYROOM

If you're lucky enough to have a bonus room in your home, make it a space where everyone wants to relax. This space is designed to work for everyone from toddlers to secondary school children and Mum and Dad.

Even a large screen works well on a modular TV stand. A companion cupboard holds stereo and other audio-video equipment, CDs, and DVDs.

Adults can work at the family computer while keeping an eye on play activities.

A blackboard wall is irresistible fun, and blackboard paint can be applied directly to drywall. Store chalk and washable erasers in buckets nearby.

A play table needs to be low enough for children but large enough for their projects. Make sure it has a surface that can be wiped clean.

Utilize awkward space beneath a low attic ceiling by filling it with valuable storage areas. For smaller children, open cubbyholes keep toys accessible and easy to put away.

MEDIA CENTRE CHECKLIST

A media centre may be as deluxe as a room with tiered seating or as simple as modular pieces arranged to set up a viewing area.

Seating Placement

Consider the amount of space you have available before racing out to buy an extra-large video screen. Viewing quality is influenced as much by distance from the screen as it is by screen size. To figure the correct distance for seating, multiply the diagonal size of the screen by 2–2.5 for HDTV and by 4 for analogue. For example, if your HDTV screen is 76 cm (30 in) across, the best range is 1.5–1.9 m (60–75 in) from the screen. A 145 cm (57 in) screen is best seen from a distance of 3–3.5 m (10–12 ft).

76 cm (30 in)

1.5–1.9 m (60–75 in)

Cupboard

Most media centre cupboards accept a wide range of screen sizes, but be sure to compare both the width and the depth of a cupboard with your TV's size.

Speakers

For a multi-speaker home cinema set-up, follow the manufacturer's guidelines for placement. In general, position left and right front speakers well apart and away from side walls, making sure the distance from you to each speaker is greater than the distance between the two speakers.

Seating

Sectional sofa units seat a crowd comfortably and efficiently, but also consider including chairs on castors or other lightweight occasional chairs in your plan, for supplemental seating.

Insulation

This is one room where rugs or wall-to-wall carpet and curtains are essential because hard surfaces distort sound.

Media has changed almost beyond imagination in the last thirty years, and the way we live with it has changed, too. Concert-quality music piped throughout the house, on-demand films appearing on flat screens, libraries of CDs and DVDs to choose from as the mood strikes – these pleasures have not only transformed the way we spend leisure time, they've also revolutionized the way that we organize our homes. Whether you have a separate room devoted to video entertainment or

MAKING ROOM
FOR MEDIA

THE BEST MEDIA STORAGE KEEPS EVERYTHING IN ORDER, MAKES THINGS EASY TO FIND IN AN INSTANT, AND FUNCTIONS AS A DECORATIVE ELEMENT IN ITS OWN RIGHT.

a large media centre that shares another room of the house, order is a must if you want these spaces to be seamlessly integrated into your home. Fortunately, specially designed furniture is now made for housing electronic equipment, and it's available in styles that complement the decor of almost any room. Most pieces include room for accessories, with spaces for video or game hardware and drawers for remote controls. It can also be fun to find antique pieces and decorative containers in which to store media equipment and accessories. With all the options currently available, it's easy to make media storage both smart and stylish.

Intuitive Storage

In a room dedicated to home entertainment, a logical plan puts everything in its place and keeps the space uncluttered and attractive.

Today's families have continually growing collections of media but limited space in which to keep them. The best way to maximize space and maintain order is with customized storage. As with storage in any room, the rule is to make it obvious and to keep it simple. Designating specific places for each kind of item you use makes organization intuitive. Keep most-used things in view and close at hand and the rest tucked away in closed storage – kids' favourite DVDs in a bin near the player, for example, and the remainder hidden in a cupboard. Adjust the heights of shelves to plainly signal what goes where, so that putting things back where they belong requires little effort.

WHY THIS ROOM WORKS

A clever storage system creates a sense of order that lets everyone who uses this media room know exactly where everything belongs.

- **ADJUSTABLE SHELVING** transforms a cupboard into storage for electronic components, disks, tapes, and photo albums. Shelves are tightly positioned and adjusted for specific contents, allowing maximum storage.

- **IDENTICAL BINDERS** holding family photographs, letters, and clippings appear more orderly because of their matching size and colour.

- **CLEAR PLASTIC BINS** for CDs keep current favourites close at hand, so you don't have to flip through your entire collection to find them.

- **OPEN SHELVING** is reserved for frequently used items that can be attractively stored.

- **A REMOTE-CONTROL HOLDER** kept in plain sight is the surest way to find controls when they're needed.

This sophisticated family room plays down its role as media central, so it's as inviting for reading or game playing as it is for TV viewing.

■ **CUBE-SHAPED SHELVING UNITS** make each display shelf a separate vignette within the larger grid, giving the wall an identity apart from its media function.

■ **A MEDIA CUPBOARD** built into the centre of the display wall is self-contained, with storage drawers stacked for easy access. Doors hide everything when the TV is not in use.

■ **ARMCHAIRS** are upholstered in washable suede, and ottomans in dark leather; both are easy-care options.

■ **A SOFT COLOUR PALETTE** allows the display wall to take centre stage.

MAKING ROOM FOR MEDIA

A Balanced Display

A handsome display wall with customized storage cupboards puts media equipment in context, surrounding it with objects and art.

Building a media cupboard into the middle of a display wall is an effective and stylish storage solution. By surrounding a television screen with a grid of shelving, equal weight is given to your other interests and pastimes, and the display remains engaging with cupboard doors open or closed. This is an especially good idea for spaces that have dual roles such as family rooms, bedrooms, and studies. Media accessories and related equipment should be stored as close to the TV as possible, so plan for extra drawers and shelves within the TV enclosure. Doors designed to slide back into the cupboard when open are also a clever idea.

For a media space that's shared with children, choose upholstery materials that are easily cleaned. Today, that includes leathers and washable suedes, so even family spaces can be furnished with sophisticated style. Cotton remains an easy-care option for upholstery, especially lightly textured chenilles and brushed twills.

Everyone has creative impulses of some kind, and having a special space in which to pursue them can be a life-changing luxury. Whether yours is a quiet art that requires little more than a pen and paper or one involving a workshop, a lathe, or a potter's wheel, having a place to pursue the task that you love is important for maintaining a balance in life. It might be as small as a desk in the corner of the kitchen or as grand as an attic studio. The important thing is, it's all yours. The best

INSPIRING CREATIVITY

THE SPACE WHERE YOU PURSUE YOUR HOBBIES AND PASSIONS SHOULD BE PERSONALLY INSPIRING. PLAN IT WITH CARE, FURNISH IT WITH COMFORT, AND INFUSE IT WITH CHARACTER.

creative spaces are a mix: half organization, half inspiration. Begin by carving out an area that's suited to the demands of your projects. Create a sense of order with well-planned furnishings, lighting, and storage, setting things up in ways that reflect the process of your craft. Then focus on the details. To ensure that you create work you're proud of, surround yourself with objects that you love and that inspire you, and provide plenty of shelf space for reference books and magazines. As much as possible, establish a sense of privacy, and bring in an armchair and other amenities that encourage you to take time out for contemplation.

A Sunlit Studio

Artists seek the purity of unfiltered daylight to practise their craft. The best creative spaces celebrate natural light and honour order.

Visual artists need – and in fact insist upon – lots of natural sunlight. Applying this preference to your own space will help to keep you energized and inspired, regardless of the project at hand.

Whether your creative space holds an easel, a writing desk, a woodworking bench, or a craft table, keep your things simply organized. Position work surfaces to take advantage of the greatest amount of daylight; northern light is ideal, but natural light of any kind tends to stimulate creativity and improve mood. To enjoy maximum sunlight from your windows, choose sheer curtains or blinds – or, if privacy allows, take full advantage of the room's light by opting for bare windows instead.

WHY THIS ROOM WORKS

Flooded with light and furnished with restraint, this calligrapher's studio gives everyday tools and works-in-progress pride of place.

■ BARE WINDOWS on two sides of the room bathe the artist's desk in natural light.

■ A WOODEN SECRETAIRE, whose small scale fits this room, provides storage space for finished drawings and art supplies and affords display space for favourite books and objects.

■ SAMPLES OF WORK, suspended from ordinary twine, catch the light and become decorative elements in their own right.

■ STACKED BOOKS on the floor contribute an offhand air and a touch of colour and leave walls unadorned.

■ AN ADJUSTABLE WORK LIGHT clips to the drawing board to supplement natural or overhead ambient light at night or on cloudy days.

Organic Design

A rustic but orderly potting shed offers valuable lessons about organization that are applicable to every kind of creative space.

"Everything in its place" is more than just an obvious catchphrase. It's a philosophy that any creative person can benefit from. Every activity has its own natural order, so pay attention to the rhythms of your work, and set up your space accordingly.

A well-organized potting shed is a perfect example. It allocates different areas for specific chores — starting seedlings, repotting plants, studying horticulture manuals or magazines — and includes carefully planned storage for all necessities: stakes, soil, fertilizer, seeds, and so on. There's a place to store tools and a place to clean them, and there's even room for valued mementos and collections, to give the space a personal touch.

WHY THIS ROOM WORKS

A weathered garden shed, fitted out with shelves, buckets, and galvanized worktops, provides a pleasant and efficient spot to spend the day gardening or organizing.

■ MULTIPLE WORK AREAS are organized as you would a kitchen. Wet areas, where soil spills over from repotting, are separated from dry sections for drawing plans or reading.

■ A GALVANIZED TUB filled with dry sand cleans hand tools with a swipe, then stores them, preventing rust.

■ WOODEN DRAWERS are partitioned to separate small ties, labels, and seed packets, which could get mislaid without an organizing system.

■ SALVAGED MATERIALS are well suited to a rough-and-ready garden shed. With a coat of white paint, they all work together visually.

■ A COLLECTION OF PADLOCKS adds wit and personality to the space.

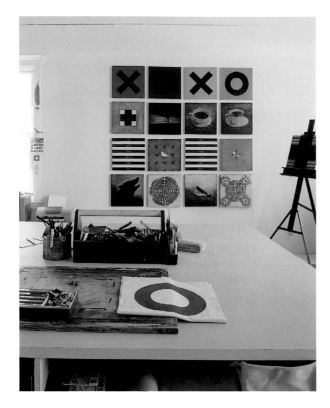

In a painter's studio, a confident use of colour, clever displays of tools and supplies, and an intelligent use of space creates a workplace that's as appealing as a gallery.

■ A PERSPEX SHEET, supported a few inches above the desktop by plumbing brackets, creates a handsome display case for smaller tools and supplies.

■ OPEN STORAGE UNITS, pushed together to form a central worktable, allow free flow of traffic and access to storage from all sides.

■ MULTIPLE STORAGE CONTAINERS are as clever as they are attractive. Cans, jars, shelves, boxes, bags – even a carpenter's toolbox – all limit clutter and contribute visual order.

INSPIRING CREATIVITY

A Painter's Eye

When setting up a studio, think like an artist. An imaginative approach to storage and space planning infuses a room with personality.

Artists are adept at finding order in chaos, and that's a talent that sometimes extends to their surroundings as well as their work. The imaginative eye of an artist turned to the physical set-up of a studio results in a room that's as distinctive as an artwork.

Finding creative and witty ways to store tools, materials, and works-in-progress brings visual harmony to a space and adds touches of whimsy. Look for inspired ideas for recycling unusual containers – mounting paint tins on a wall for in and out boxes, for example – or interesting ways to create storage, such as using a child's chair to hold frequently used materials. Think creatively about space, consolidating storage in ways that make the most of the room you have. Organizing storage along walls gives you room to move freely in the centre of the space; focussing storage in a central workstation allows access from all sides and creates aisles for passage around it.

You don't need a trip to the woods or the seaside to gain the benefits of being outdoors. It's never been easier to enjoy the open air. Simply look to your own garden. Whatever size garden or patio you have, make the best use of it by creating a space that invites you to get outside and relax. Outdoor areas are often the last to get decorating attention, but they shouldn't be. Make them as comfortable as the rest of your home, carrying your sense of style through to outdoor furnishings,

ENJOYING THE
OPEN AIR

THE NATURAL RESPONSE TO FINE WEATHER IS TO GET OUT AND ENJOY IT. MAKE THE MOST OF THE SEASON BY CUSTOMIZING OUTDOOR SPACES FOR CAREFREE RELAXATION.

whether country casual, ocean-liner chic, or cabana cool. Fashionable weather-resistant fabrics allow you to co-ordinate accessories just as you would in your living room. What are your favourite open-air pleasures? Plan spaces that make it easy for you to pursue the activity – or inactivity – that you love. Look for ways to add comfort: seating arranged for easy conversation, ample table surfaces for drinks and food, and plump cushions that encourage lounging. Finishing touches like table linen, candles, lanterns, and accessories give an outdoor space your personal stamp, while extra towels, throws, and cushions make guests feel right at home.

Cabana Style

Thoughtfully furnished, a poolside cabana can become everyone's favourite room throughout the entire warm-weather season.

The key to relaxed outdoor living is combining beauty and comfort with the benefits of easy care. That means providing welcoming seating and gracious amenities for everyone, but making sure that furnishings can weather heavy use. Choose practical furniture crafted from hardwoods that stand up to the elements. Supply plenty of cushions in bright colours that celebrate the outdoors; choose washable or weather-friendly fabrics to ensure that they'll stay fresh-looking all season long. Create inviting places to escape the sun with weather-resistant canvas patio umbrellas or awnings. Stock up on durable tableware, and add thoughtful touches like rolled towels and water bottles.

WHY THIS ROOM WORKS

Designed around two separate areas, this poolside set-up offers an irresistible invitation for guests to enjoy themselves in the sun or to gather and relax in the shade.

■ WEATHER-RESISTANT LOUNGERS, fitted with cushions covered in terry-cloth loose covers in bright colours, are equipped with built-in beverage trays. A milkman's basket filled with flip-flops invites guests to help themselves.

■ CANVAS GARDEN UMBRELLAS near the pool provide protection when bathers are ready for some shade. A poolside pavilion with canvas curtains and comfortable seating offers a place to gather and snack out of the sun.

■ TEAK BENCHES double as cocktail tables and can be moved outdoors as needed for parties.

■ COLOURFUL PLASTIC TRAYS are a practical choice for a poolside setting. Frozen lemon and lime slices are tasty alternatives to ice cubes.

An Urban Escape

A small balcony can be every bit as relaxing as a large garden. Create a piece of paradise in even the tiniest of outdoor spots.

City dwellers need as much open-air relaxation as their country counterparts. Luckily, it's fairly simple to create a serene green space on a patio or balcony. First, look at scale. The furniture and plant containers you choose should be appropriately sized for the setting. A few well-chosen smaller-sized pieces can give the impression of a fully furnished space, and even a single row of leafy perennials can provide a sense of enclosure. Next, choose durable, lightweight materials; plastic containers on castors make it easy to rotate plants as needed to give each time in the sun. Finally, don't forget lighting; several solar-powered lights staked in the planters add drama and give a garden a finished look at night.

WHY THIS ROOM WORKS

This small city balcony has the impact of a larger garden, thanks to its clever sense of proportion. Plants and furnishings fill the space without overwhelming it.

■ LUSH PLANTINGS arranged in lightweight plastic pots soften the balcony's edges and create the look of a border garden.

■ WEATHERED PLANKS add to the natural look of the balcony; they can be laid on top of concrete to give a city patio a more rustic look.

■ SOLAR-POWERED lanterns and orbs cast a soft glow by night. Requiring only six hours of sunlight to recharge, solar lights are as environmentally wise as they are aesthetically pleasing.

■ A POWDER-COATED METAL TABLE is weather resistant and scaled for a small space. A seagrass slipper chair, moved outdoors in good weather, provides a soft spot to relax. Seagrass pieces used inside the house give a room a relaxed feel.

The charms of this boathouse are enhanced by low-maintenance, high-comfort furnishings and personal accents that play off a nautical theme.

■ **A PALE WASH OF PAINT** on the simple plywood walls unifies the space and makes it seem larger; it's also a good foil for brighter accents.

■ **PEGBOARD PANELS** define a walk-in cupboard for storing boating and water-sports equipment, and provide extra room for family members' belongings.

■ **FAMILY PHOTOS AND MEMORABILIA** give the space the personality and style of an indoor room.

■ **BOATING HOOKS** double as towel and tackle hooks and even make handles for an improvised serving tray.

ENJOYING THE OPEN AIR

A Boathouse Family Room

Furnished with the comforts of an indoor room, an open-air boathouse is a perfect retreat for a family that lives at water's edge.

When there's nowhere you'd rather be than on the water, why go back to the house to relax after you've docked the boat? Turn the protected space of a boat-house into a family room and extend afternoons on the water into evenings at its edge. All you need are a few comfortable places to stretch out on — sectional pieces are wonderfully adaptable — and some personal touches that connect the space to home and family.

Let the bright colours and distinctive shapes of the boating gear inform the decor. Choose lightweight furnishings that are easily moved to storage or back to the house at season's end, and use tough, mildew-resistant fabric for seat coverings. Create a spot to stow equipment like skis and fishing rods, but don't make a fuss about hiding it all from view; the most important views here are the ones looking out to nature.

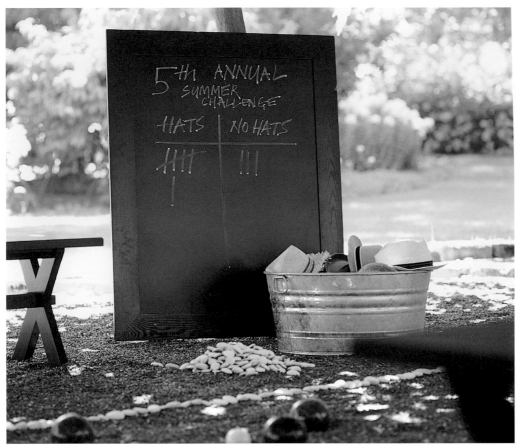

A Shady Grove

A tree-shaded haven for garden parties, get-togethers, and lawn games is a refined but easy addition to a spacious garden.

If you've ever admired those big luncheon parties so often seen in foreign films, set in outdoor groves and accompanied by games of boules, you're not alone. The good news is, that's an atmosphere that can be reproduced in your own garden. Fast-growing trees planted in rows quickly create an outdoor "room" that can be enjoyed for generations to come.

As a landscaping upgrade, this is one of the easiest designs to start from scratch, and one of the most dramatic. Choose a spot, and plant equal-length rows of fast-growers such as poplars or willows. A simple crushed gravel surface, well suited to shade, games, and foot traffic, completes the design.

WHY THIS ROOM WORKS

Finishing touches turn this essentially simple setting into a picture-perfect location for family reunions and long afternoons at the table or on the games court.

■ A CRISP LINEN TABLECLOTH and plump cushions on the wooden benches contribute to the festive atmosphere. They make even a rustic picnic table look luxurious.

■ CERAMIC PLATES instead of paper, and proper cutlery instead of plastic, are small amenities that make guests feel genuinely indulged.

■ EXTRA CHAIRS, arranged in pairs and groups, encourage intimate conversations or can be pulled up to the ends of the table.

■ HURRICANE LAMPS set firmly in gravel, and lights strung from overhead branches cast a magical spell over evenings outdoors.

■ STRAW HATS are tongue-in-cheek accessories for an afternoon of old-fashioned fun and games.

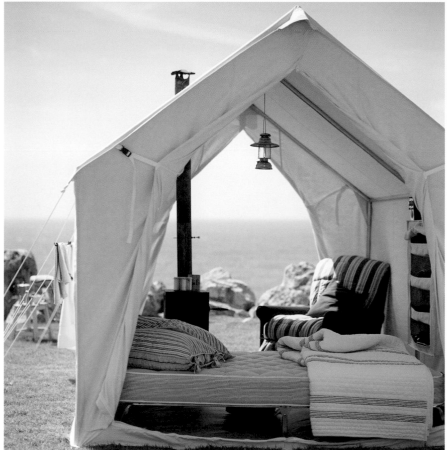

NAPPING IN THE SHADE IS PURE WARM-WEATHER BLISS. PICK YOUR SPOT AND SET UP A COSY RETREAT FOR AN AFTERNOON SNOOZE.

An all-weather chaise longue, *above left*, is a welcome sight for swimmers ready for some rest and relaxation. Position it beneath an overhang or patio umbrella and dress it with waterproof cushions and a light blanket to ward off a chill.

A canvas tent pavilion, *left*, is its own outdoor room. To make it comfortable for the entire summer, furnish it with amenities like a folding camp bed, a portable stove, and plenty of cushions.

A lightweight portable bed, *above*, makes setting up a garden sleeping station a two-minute affair. All you have to do is grab your folding lounger and a cushion and blanket, and head for the nearest shady spot.

A classic hammock, *right*, is a summertime staple that's hard to resist. At the beginning of the season, string one up between a pair of shade trees or on a covered veranda, and you'll have a perfect spot for napping in the breeze.

COLOUR

"COLOUR HAS THE POWER TO CALM, COMFORT, ENERGIZE, AND INSPIRE. I WANT TO BRING COLOUR TO EVERY ROOM OF MY HOME AND HAVE IT WORK BEAUTIFULLY."

Choosing Colour

If you're looking for a colour change, begin by identifying a range of hues that you respond to. Within these pages, you'll find a plan for harmonizing colour throughout your home.

Some of our favourite wall colours fall into two broad categories: neutral and earthy colours, and saturated and soft ones. Within each category, the palettes we favour tend to be muted: more dusty than bright, warm but not hot, comfortable rather than dramatic. These are colours that speak with resonance but never shout, reflecting our philosophy that the colours you choose should enhance, not overpower, the furnishings in a room. The colour palettes featured throughout these pages are just that:

impactful, though not agressive, and graceful, though not affected. In addition, the plans for organizing these palettes show you how to create an integrated system of colour throughout your home and how to highlight existing decorative elements.

Even if you're only painting one room, it's helpful to begin by mapping out a colour plan for the entire house. You'll find that creating a soothing flow of colours from room to room establishes a unified environment and simplifies the process of choosing colours for each space. Use the examples on the opposite page as a starting point. Because colour printing processes can alter the way colour appears, be sure to test any colour that you are considering, especially as the light changes throughout the day.

LIGHT AND VALUE

A hue may have a whole range of tones that appear lighter or darker, and seem to change in different lighting.

■ NATURAL LIGHT AND SHADOW transform the appearance of a paint colour into graduated values of the original, as seen above; they almost appear to be different colours. Make sure you test a colour in both daylight and artificial light to see its range.

■ VALUE denotes the lightness or darkness of a hue. Above, lighter values (tints) of the wall colour appear at the top of the row of brushstrokes, and move to darker values (shades) at the bottom. Choosing different values of one colour that you love is an effective way to co-ordinate colours from room to room.

BUILDING A COLOUR PLAN

Planning colour for the entire house makes a more cohesive statement because each colour is supported by others in a harmonious palette.

■ HUES OF THE SAME VALUE are used to help unify different wall colours that will be seen together, such as the living room, library, and hallway.

■ IN THE HALLWAY, choose a colour that makes a smooth transition, to harmonize with adjoining rooms.

■ THE LIBRARY'S WARM TAUPE calls for a complementary lighter grey in the kitchen and breakfast area.

■ THE VERANDA has walls painted the same colour as the adjacent kitchen. To further connect the spaces, the blue-green of the kitchen cupboards is repeated on the ceiling of the veranda.

■ THE DINING ROOM stays within warm neutrals but appears more tan than grey.

■ THE TRIM is painted throughout with a slightly warm white.

COLOUR IN AN OPEN PLAN

When several different rooms or spaces are seen together, it's especially important to co-ordinate a palette for the entire house.

■ START WITH ONE COLOUR that you love. For example, this plan begins with the deep rust colour used in the dining room. A lighter hue is used in the library across the hallway, to temper the dining room's dramatic colour.

■ SATURATED COLOURS like deep rust and the darker brown used in the powder room are often better reserved for areas that are used occasionally rather than seen every day.

■ CONTINUE THE HALLWAY COLOUR into the living room, as a directional clue. Here a medium-range taupe complements adjoining rooms.

■ CHOOSE A NEUTRAL COLOUR for a central space and build upon it. A light stone colour anchors the kitchen, the taupe gives the living room a little more weight, and the cream used in the family room plays up its spaciousness.

■ TRIM COLOUR is a very pure white that affords a crisp look.

Neutral and earthy colours are hues based in nature that evoke a grounded sense of well-being – stone, cream, sky, jade, terracotta, and mustard are all good examples. Our favourite neutral colours are found at the lighter end of this group, our earthy hues at the darker end (see the individual palettes on the following pages). Neutral colours bring a sense of tranquillity to a room, and they're also a great base upon which you can layer more intense colours. Adding touches of warmer hues gives depth to

NEUTRAL
AND EARTHY COLOURS

AGREEABLE AND EASY TO LIVE WITH, THESE TONES ARE THE MOST VERSATILE COLOUR CHOICES. FOR A NATURALLY SOOTHING HOME, TAKE ADVANTAGE OF THEIR RELAXING EFFECT.

a room; in general, warm neutrals like creams and tans pair well with red and yellow accents. Cooler neutrals like greys and whites are best accented with crisp blues and hues from the cooler end of the palette. Earthy colours are a natural extension of neutrals but tend to be richer and warmer. Their intensity can be played up or down to suit your taste and the amount of light in a room. Use a stronger earthy colour on just a single wall, for instance, if you want a quieter effect or if the room tends to be dark. Add some spark to deep earthy hues with clear, sharp colours such as chartreuse or sunny yellow to bring a contemporary attitude to a space.

Selecting a Neutral Colour Palette

In the world of colour, neutral does not mean bland. Neutrals encompass a whole range of subtle variations and have hints of blue, green, red, or yellow. A room is given elegance and depth by layering closely related hues.

Neutrals are the chameleons of the colour world, an almost infinite range of whites, greys, and tans that can run warm or cool and that change in response to subtle changes in light throughout the day. Depending upon a neutral's colour value – how light or dark its shade is – it can serve as either a dominant or a background colour. Used together in a variety of values, neutrals add quiet texture. Because they carry the flow between rooms with more subtlety than any other palette, they are a natural choice for open-plan houses.

Neutral paint colours all have a base that includes red, yellow, green, or blue; this undertone will be more apparent when the paint is on your walls. For instance, a true tan has a hint of red in it, khaki leans towards green, and another tan may have yellow highlights. Similarly, grey appears warmer or cooler depending on how much red or blue is in its base. While it's hard to discern the difference when looking at a single colour, it's easy to see when you put several neutrals together.

When choosing colours, be sure to consider the tones of wood floors, built-in cupboards, carpeting, and fixed architectural features such as stone or brickwork in the surrounding space – oak, for example, is enhanced by warmer tones. Choose a wall colour that harmonizes with the undertones of the room's materials, or select a contrasting hue to highlight their colours.

A NEUTRAL MOOD BOARD

Gathering samples of colours and objects that appeal to you and creating a "mood board" is a good place to start when choosing colour.

■ **A MUTED PALETTE** requires an especially lively mix of textures to enhance the room's visual interest. Incorporate velvets, linen, and other textural weaves for variety.

■ **LOOK FOR NATURAL ELEMENTS** like rocks, shells, straw, or distressed wood; rougher textures enhance an informal attitude in a neutral space.

■ **CREATE CONTRAST** by juxtaposing warm with cool. You don't need bright colours to add variety – use a pale lavender-blue to contrast with a warm grey or tan, for example.

Perfectly White, *left*

Whites are the ultimate neutrals. Here a creamy white wall colour is matched with a range of warm white hues in furnishings and accessories and complemented with accent pieces like burnished wood and supple leather. Though the room is predominantly monochromatic, it reads as warm and welcoming, thanks to a careful balance of highlights and undertones.

Paired Colours, *right*

A warmer tan wall in a bedroom is well matched with a pale yellow in the adjoining hallway, which picks up its undertones. When planning colour, be sure to consider the view from one room to the next. The golden tones of the wood flooring and the intriguing bedside table also harmonize well with the paint colours. Paint on the mouldings and cupboards is a rich white that, along with the white silk and cotton bedding, provides a crisp counterpoint to the warm scheme.

Handsome Understatement, *left*

Warm grey is anything but drab when it's used in a sophisticated mix. Paired with deep brown wooden cupboards, stone worktops, and neat white trim and window treatments, this bathroom's wall colour is subdued and calming – just what's called for in a room designed for restoration and relaxation. The space's sleekness is nicely balanced with a rich range of textures: a terry-cloth cover on the window seat, stacks of towels, a braided rug, and a display of sponges.

Selecting an Earthy Colour Palette

Introducing the organic colours of the earth into your home is a simple way to ground it in a sense of natural warmth. The deep, beautiful hues of nature are timeless and are consistently a pleasure to live with.

Earthy colours are those found in nature: charcoal, chestnut, ochre, persimmon, plum, terracotta. They are elemental, familiar, and reassuring. Though our selected earth tones tend to be darker than neutrals and make more of a visual statement, they have a similar muted quality. We especially like these hues because of the sense of comfort they bring to a room, and also for their versatility: earth tones are neither masculine nor feminine. Although these colours naturally complement rustic or informal rooms, they

also lend themselves to more refined living rooms, forming a perfect backdrop for jewel-toned upholstery. Earth tones are a good choice in rooms that feature natural materials such as wooden beams or flooring, or stone or brick fireplaces. They are also well suited to spaces that see everyday use like family rooms or bedrooms, where the snug, cocooning effect of deeper shades is especially welcome. In a media room, using a darker earth tone cuts glare and makes onscreen colours appear brighter.

Despite earth tones' richness, they work well with a wide variety of accent colours. They look sophisticated, crisp, and tailored when paired with a creamy white trim; for a layered, more organic feel, use a more muted shade of the main room colour or another earthy hue for mouldings or accents.

EARTHY INSPIRATIONS

When gathering samples for an earthy palette, remember to explore a wide range of hues – don't limit yourself to browns and terracotta.

■ LOOK TO NATURE for inspiration: even an earthy landscape often contains vibrant splashes of bolder colour. Mix some stronger colours into your palette.

■ KEEP TEXTURE IN MIND when selecting colour. The same hue in buttery leather evokes a different feeling in linen or chenille, where texture warms the hue.

■ REMEMBER PATTERN: Whether seen in the grid of a solid-coloured basketweave or in the repeated motifs of a printed pattern fabric, pattern is a powerful element in any colour scheme.

Strong and Grounded, *left*

Earth tones are frequently thought of as tending towards browns and reds, but blues and greens are also drawn from nature, and are vital parts of an earthy palette. Here, a deep grey-blue is a cooling complement to the red tones of the wood, and is picked up in the kilim-design cushions and rugs. The relatively dark value of the wall colour is perfect for creating a soothing and sheltering atmosphere in this reading nook, which is part of a large open-plan space.

Calm and Collected, *right*

This handsome study is appealingly lively yet subdued, due to its thoughtful balance of colour. A tan on the walls, accented with fresh white trim and tailored Roman blinds, gives the room a spacious feel. In contrast, deeper tones predominate on the floor and in the furnishings, creating a dynamic play between the lighter walls and the darker central areas: the deep browns and earth tones ground the space while the tan-and-white walls lift and expand it.

Naturally Sophisticated, *right*

An earthy palette gives a sophisticated space natural appeal. Creamy coffee walls in a smart and casual living room look elegant with fresh white trim. Natural materials and accent pieces bring in complementary earth tones and add layers of texture — chenille, suede, leather, wood, and matchstick blinds at the windows. A burst of red on the sofa punctuates the palette and enlivens the colour scheme.

Some people believe that no room is truly complete without a dash of red. If you're looking for a colour that makes a statement, red is pretty much the front-runner, and is a perfect example of what saturated colour can do for a space. Strong colour is a wake-up call, a bold bid for attention that usually works just as intended. For those whose preference for a power punch tends towards deep violet, emerald, indigo, or tangerine, the principle holds equally true, and these hues can deliver the same impact.

SATURATED
AND SOFT COLOURS

FOR THOSE WHO LOVE STRONG COLOUR AND WANT TO INTRODUCE IT INTO THEIR HOME, HARMONY LIES IN SELECTING A BOLD COLOUR AND LAYERING WITH CONFIDENCE.

The crucial factors in using a saturated colour are the strength and clarity of the hue and the confidence with which you use it. The colours we've chosen to call "soft" are not quite the opposite of saturated; they're more like their kissing cousins. Soft colours are romantic, flattering, and enduring, and include a range drawn from nature's gentler hues: cerulean, lavender, lemon, periwinkle, rose. They layer well with neutrals or with other soft hues of the same value. Soft colours have always been natural choices for the bathroom, bedroom, and nursery, but you'll also find that they're flattering and fresh in the living room, dining area, or kitchen, too.

Selecting a Saturated Colour Palette

When it comes to using eye-popping colour in their homes, most people either wouldn't dream of it or they can't imagine life without it. Bold colour is an adventure worth taking, but it requires careful decision making.

For those in search of drama in a room, nothing beats rich, wall-to-wall saturated colour. Before you take the plunge, though, try a simple test. Mark off an area of 30–120 sq cm (5–17 sq in) and paint a colour swatch on your wall so you can see how the hue looks under different light conditions, including lamplight. If you are trying to decide between two or more colours, paint swatches in each colour to compare. Live with the colours for at least a week to see how they agree with you.

An increasingly popular choice, suited to even more conservative tastes, is to highlight a single wall, a hallway, or an architectural feature with bold colour. This trick brings instant energy to a room and has been known to make converts of even the most timid home colourists. Another alternative is to start with a less frequently used space such as a dedicated dining room, where the intensity of the colour will have a lesser impact than in a room that you use daily.

Whatever size room you choose to paint, balance bold colour with lighter elements: white trim or accents in pale or neutral hues, light-coloured rugs or wood floors, furniture upholstered in muted tones. Above all, take care not to overdo saturated colour. Stick to just one vibrant colour in a room, and consider the views from adjoining rooms as well.

SATURATED INSPIRATIONS

You're not likely to use a whole range of bold colours within one room. Find samples and swatches that appeal to you that also co-ordinate with other hues in your decorating plan.

■ PLAN THE AREA for which you're choosing a saturated colour carefully, whether an entire room or just a feature wall. Take into account the impact that amount of colour will have on the room.

■ CHOOSE COLOURS for accent pieces that carry colour out into the rest of the room. Cushions, throws, and other small accessories, whether solid or patterned, are essential parts of a colour plan.

■ CONSIDER FURNITURE FINISHES when choosing colours, too. Light woods play well off saturated colours; darker ones intensify a colour's effect.

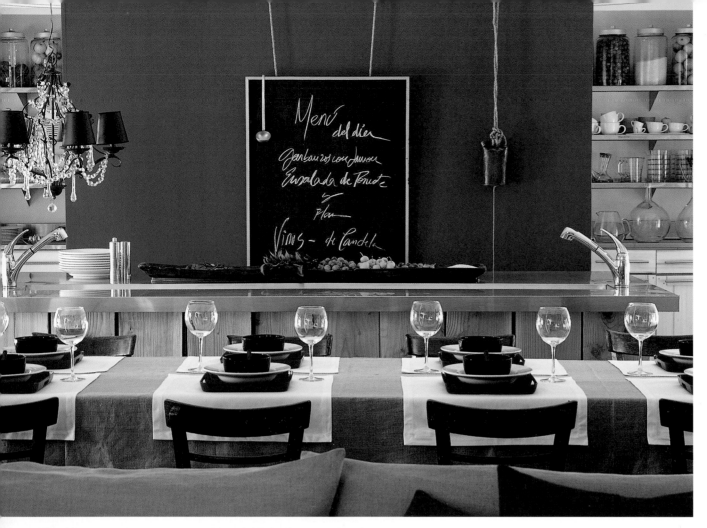

Well-Staged Drama, *left*

A partial wall like this one, which screens the working part of a kitchen from an open-plan dining area, is a prime candidate for saturated colour. Highlighting one single wall with a bold hue is a shrewd way to enjoy the benefits of strong colour without being overwhelmed by it. Carry the colour through the room with decorative accessories like cushions, table settings, or other accent pieces. Red is a perennial favourite, prized for its energizing appeal.

Pure and Vibrant, *right*

Yellows are often used for a cheery and charming effect — think of yellow-and-white summer cottages — but a saturated yellow like the marigold featured here can evoke a more cosmopolitan air. If choosing a strong wall colour for an entire room, especially a living room, it's often safest to stay away from extremes of colour and choose a midtone that delivers impact but still enhances the room's furnishings and lets them retain focus.

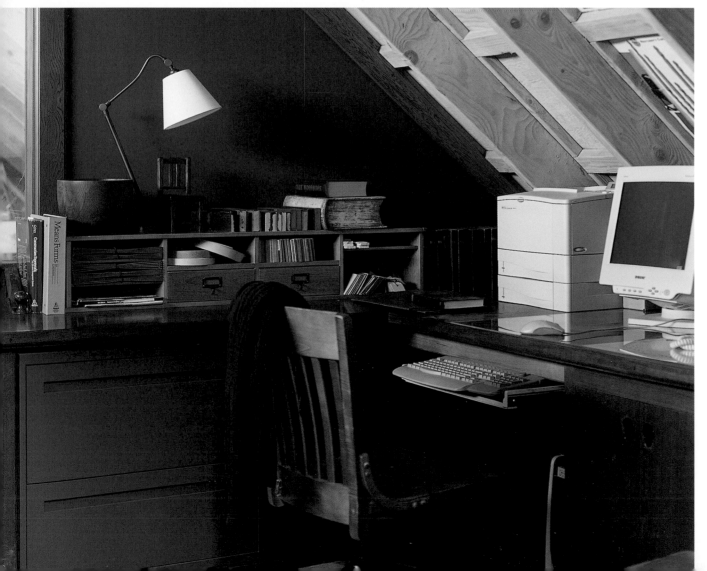

Snug and Stylish, *left*

Rich saturated hues work as well in smaller spaces as they do in larger ones, especially if you're aiming to create a secluded spot for work or for reading and relaxing. This attic office has a cosy and inviting feel with its plum walls and warm wooden furnishings. White-stained woodwork is a smart choice for breaking up and balancing the stronger hues and deeper tones. An abundance of daylight is welcome in any room but is especially important in a room painted in saturated colour.

Selecting a Soft Colour Palette

Not to be confused with pastels, soft colours have a crisp appeal all their own. They're also more versatile than you might think, pairing as successfully with stainless steel as they do with white panelling.

Once relegated to the bedroom and bathroom, soft colours are now used to make the living room, dining room, and kitchen look fresh. The way we decorate rooms with soft tones has been updated as well. Pairing a soft wall colour with floral fabric is a timeless favourite, but the same colour set off by crisp white linen upholstery produces an effect that's every bit as welcoming. To make soft colours work in any part of your home, choose slightly greyer counterparts to pastels, which might come off as too sweet or bright.

Like saturated colours, soft colours can benefit from being finished with clean white trim. You can also try tinting white paint with the wall colour that you've chosen, to create a paler version of the primary hue for use on trim or ceilings. Using graduated values of a colour that you love can help you co-ordinate adjacent areas. For instance, add white to the colour you've chosen for the bedroom and use it on the bathroom walls. Or you might choose a slightly darker shade of the bedroom colour for the adjacent hallway. Paint professionals can work with you to assure a pleasing difference in values.

Soft colours work well with silver-toned accessories, from your grandmother's silver to contemporary steel photo frames. They're also as striking a backdrop for black-and-white photographs as they are for bright artworks and objects in contrasting colours.

SOFT INSPIRATIONS

When choosing soft colours, think "fresh" rather than "delicate". Find colours that recall early spring and summer mornings, and their dusky counterparts.

■ CHOOSE FURNISHINGS that don't necessarily match the wall colour but instead are interesting variations or attractive complements.

■ NATURAL MATERIALS like wicker, raffia, linen, and sisal are particularly attractive in a room decorated in a soft palette.

■ CONSIDER COLOUR VALUE: Find a hue for a wall colour, then choose colours in lighter or darker values of that hue for trim, accents, and fabrics. For contrast, if the wall colour is warm, choose some cooler complementary hues and include them in the mix, or vice versa.

Simple Pleasure, *left*

Sunny flaxen walls pair with milky white trim and warm pine furniture for an enduring colour combination that's a pleasure to live with every day. Soft colours are seen more and more these days in living and dining rooms because they add energy and colour to a space but are quiet enough to be a flexible backdrop for your decor. The simplicity of this colour palette is complemented by a similar restraint in furnishings.

Neat and Clean, *right*

Sky blue and white combine to give this tidy laundry room a breezy appeal. The palette is refreshing yet calm, and it welcomes accents in other complementary soft colours – bottle and spring greens, pale grey-blues, creamy beiges – as well as materials such as warm wicker and cool metal.

Fresh Appeal, *right*

Soft green hues like this celery offer another lively but adaptable range of colours to choose from. According to colour theorists, green is seen as calming, but paired with white cupboards and trim, it also brings a gentle energy to a room. In this neat and tidy family room, the palette is warmed by natural wood, wicker, sisal, and cotton twill, and punctuated with a few bursts of stronger colour in the scatter cushions and accent pieces.

The special virtues of pattern are well known: patterns give a room its character and depth, and help define its overall style. They express exuberance, come in countless varieties – dots, florals, graphics, paisleys, and stripes of all sizes – and effortlessly multiply their effect when mixed in artistic combination. Because they can be used to great advantage in small quantities, patterns are also immensely practical. The punch they bring to a room frees you to opt for solid coloured fabrics for basic

PATTERN
AND TEXTURE

PATTERN AND TEXTURE ARE THE UNDERAPPRECIATED SUPPORTING PLAYERS OF HOME DESIGN, ADDING INTEREST AND PERSONALITY WITHOUT STEALING THE SCENE.

upholstery and curtains, and to choose cushions, throws, and rugs in more daring designs for fresh impact or an occasional update. Texture, pattern's close relation, enhances visual appeal in a room, upping its luxury quotient with the addition of brushed canvas, fur, silk, and velvet, or relaxing more formal furnishings by contrasting them with a rustic basket, handwoven rug, or stone bowl. Bringing texture into a room is like inviting good conversationalists to a dinner party. Just as you'd gather a mix of interesting friends at the table to spark one another, bring together multiple textures in your home to create an intriguing atmosphere.

Adding Pattern and Texture

One of the pleasures of using pattern and texture in a room is the licence it gives you to indulge your taste for variety and whimsy while maintaining an overall sense of harmony.

As with most seemingly effortless effects, the secret to successfully mixing pattern and texture lies in understanding some basic principles before you begin tweaking them. The photo grid on the right illustrates a simple but almost foolproof method to help you gain confidence in mixing patterns. Group fabrics into categories: solids, overall prints, stripes, geometric prints, and organic prints (shown here in rows of yellows, blues, and reds). When choosing furnishings for a room, look for patterns that share a common colour, and pick one from each of these categories. For a livelier effect, you can stray outside the colour range, but then it's best to find patterns whose sizes are closely matched. Solid fabrics that read as pattern are also great choices because they harmonize effortlessly: brocades, damasks, herringbones. Smocked, ruched, pleated, or embroidered fabrics also read as pattern and are easy to include in a mix.

Translate these same principles to the entire room. For example, you might have a mix of solid upholstery, geometric rugs, and subtly striped curtains. You might add side chairs upholstered in a small overall pattern and scatter cushions of an organic pattern.

Once you have your furniture in place, begin to explore textural variations that add visual interest. Start with contrasts: shiny silk with matt velvet; nubby chenille with smooth leather; glazed porcelain with rustic wood. Try out different patterns and textures, adding and subtracting a piece at a time until you've got the perfect mix.

Solids
The solid piece of the mix may be your upholstery or bed covering, whether classic linen or soft leather. For greater depth, look for solid fabrics with strong tactile interest: mohair, chenille, matelassé, or ruched or pleated fabrics.

Overall Prints
Small motifs repeated over large areas create overall pattern, which is surprisingly versatile when used in a mix. Quilted and embroidered fabrics, particularly in small repeated designs, display pattern through texture.

Stripes

Perhaps the most versatile of all patterns, stripes come in a great range of widths and colours, from narrow ticking to broad awning stripes, making them friendly companions to many other fabric patterns.

Geometric Prints

Another extremely easy mixer, geometrics include an enormous range of patterns, from simple checks and plaids to the more complicated angular patterns found in kilim rugs and upholstery and carpet materials.

Organic Prints

Flowing vines, florals, and many other patterns that take inspiration from the natural world mix well with many other patterns and bring vitality to a grouping. Organic patterns add richness and romance to a setting.

Layered Comfort, *left*
This rich mix of patterns and textures conjures the feel of an exotic spa. Deftly juxtaposing smooth and polished surfaces with rough and honed ones, the decor demonstrates how texture and pattern play off each other – the geometry of the kilims is balanced with the repeated pattern of the iron grille, while the filmy voile at the window contrasts with the rough stone and cast-earth walls. Furnishings are harmonized by their earthy and jewel-tone colours.

Quiet Pattern, *right*
A subtle combination of patterns brings an elegant sophistication to a grouping. A mix of cushions with their small repeated motifs is united by their similar colours; the carpet plays out the colours in a larger motif. The throw's nubby weave adds another layer of texture and also reads as pattern. Contrasts in texture also add appeal – the sheen of silk and leather against the soft basketweave of the upholstery.

Easy Comfort, *left*
Layers of texture make even a simple, casual room more interesting and engaging. Here, a cream, blue, and brown palette looks polished and inviting thanks to the understated mix of patterns and textures. The visible weave of the sofa fabric contrasts with the plush pick-stitch quilt and downy throw. Cushions play by the rules and mix a solid, stripe, and pattern, but all stay within the palette.

LIGHT

"SUNLIGHT CHANGES THE WHOLE FEELING OF MY HOME. I WANT A BALANCED MIX OF LIGHTING THAT SUSTAINS THAT WARMTH BUT LETS ME CREATE DIFFERENT MOODS."

Natural light is universally welcomed in our everyday lives. We still turn the clocks back each autumn to buy back that single hour of morning sun. In the home, windows, skylights, French windows, and doors with side lights are the primary portals of daylight, and they're the best starting points for developing a lighting plan for your house. When choosing window treatments, think not only of their decorative effects, but look at them also as opportunities to control the

WORKING WITH
NATURAL LIGHT

NATURAL SUNLIGHT INFUSES A ROOM WITH LIFE. USE IT AS A POWERFUL TOOL TO TRANSFORM COLOURS, WARM THE ATMOSPHERE, AND LIGHTEN THE HEART.

quantity and quality of illumination in your home. There's something comforting about the dappled patterns thrown across furnishings by sunlight peeking through Venetian blinds; the sheerest of fabrics at the window filters the sun's rays while still preserving views beyond. On those mornings when you don't want sunbeams breaking into your bedroom, lined curtains or blackout blinds save the day. Beyond the control of light, fabric curtains also help soften rooms full of hard surfaces, such as the dining room. When a room calls for restraint, blinds and shutters offer tailored alternatives, and also contribute a sense of architectural character.

Fabric at the Window

Well-chosen curtains can do for a room what a colourful scarf does for an everyday outfit. Use simple panels of fabric to add instant texture and colour.

Simple fabric panels hanging gracefully from iron or wooden rods are the standard for window treatments today. Not only do they make decorating simpler than treatments with pelmets and swags, they also are less expensive, and there's a broad selection available ready-made. Use them to add colour and textural interest to any room.

Curtains can be lined or unlined, paired with sheers, or hung on their own. Unlined curtains have a loose, natural drape and allow some daylight to filter through them. Combining sheer panels of voile or organdy with opaque curtains

provides the maximum amount of privacy and flexibility in controlling the amount of light that a room gets. Translucent fabrics like linen, organdy, and voile gently filter light without blocking views. Heavier fabrics such as velvet are more formal looking but effectively block sun in summer and draughts in winter.

Curtains in a solid colour or understated stripes create a more enduring background for a room than curtains with a showy print. Choosing a curtain colour in a shade close to that of the walls is a sophisticated way to dress up a room. Single-toned damasks or raw silks add textural interest and natural elegance to an otherwise spare setting. Whatever your choice of fabric, hanging curtains high on a wall is a simple way to add height and grace to a room.

MEASURING FOR CURTAINS

A good rule of thumb is to mount rods 10 cm (4 in) above a window frame. You can add visual height to a room by mounting a rod just below the ceiling moulding (or ceiling). Another attractive option is to place the rod midway between ceiling and top of window.

■ **ROD LENGTH:** A pole or rod should extend 7.5–15 cm (3–6 in) beyond both sides of the window frame if you want open curtains to completely clear the window. Always decide on the type of rod, its mounted height, and hanging method (see opposite page) before measuring for curtains, because these affect final measurements.

■ **CURTAIN LENGTH:** Measure the distance from the rod to the floor (B). Floor-length curtains should clear the floor by 2.5 cm (1 in). For a puddle effect, add 15–20 cm (6–8 in) to the rod-to-floor measurement. For curtains that just break at the floor, add 7.5–10 cm (3–4 in). Factor in the size of the pole and rings, tie tops, or clips, as these can add 2.5 cm (1 in) or more to the hanging length.

■ **CURTAIN WIDTH:** Measure the width of the window including the frame (A) and multiply by 1 for a tailored look, by 1.5 for a standard look, or by 3 for a full look. The lighter the fabric, the more you'll need to achieve a full look.

Sheer panels, *left,* are gathered at the bottoms and pinned up to the centre with a ribbon, a simple way to dress up lightweight curtains.

Track-Rod Mount

A rod that contains a track allows you to draw curtains easily with string controls on the side. Utilitarian in looks, track-rods are concealed by the curtain heading (in this case, pinched pleats).

Pole Pocket Mount

A fabric pocket across the top of a panel creates a channel through which a pole is inserted. This style calls for a full look, and because it can be difficult to draw curtains, it is most suitable for sheers.

Ring-Top and Pole Mount

This style is a favourite for its casual look and also for the ease with which curtains can be opened and closed. Almost any type of fabric works with this informal mounting.

Sheer Fabrics

Fabrics such as voile, organdy, and lightweight "handkerchief" linen offer an airy feel. They reduce glare while maintaining the view, but they do not provide much privacy at night.

Unlined Fabrics

Medium-weight fabrics such as linen or cotton do not necessarily require lining. Unlined cottons and linen offer both privacy and light, and are a good choice for a more casual look.

Lined Fabrics

Heavier fabrics such as raw silk and velvet are traditionally lined to help screen out light and noise. Plan for a 7.5 cm (3 in) overlap in the middle to create a continuous screen across the window.

Border Upgrade

Ready-made curtains can be customized with a distinctive sewn-on border. A border may be a contrasting solid fabric or print and should not exceed one-third of the curtain's length.

Contrast Lining

A patterned or contrasting-colour lining adds panache to solid-colour curtains. It's not necessary to line the entire curtain; a 45 cm (18 in) strip along the centre edges will give the look of a full lining.

Contrast Edging

A band of ribbon or a strip of fabric in a colour contrasting to the curtain fabric can be sewn onto the edges of panels to give them a tailored finish and add an extra touch of colour.

Blinds and Shutters

Generally more casual than curtains, this group of sleek window coverings can be used in conjunction with curtains for maximum control of light and privacy.

Sometimes even the most informal curtains just don't work in a given room or at a particular window. It may be because of an architectural element – a built-in window seat or a radiator, for example – or because of practical concerns or style preferences. Children's rooms, for instance, are best served by contained window treatments, especially blackout blinds, which are a great help with early bedtimes. (Look for a cordless lift option, which is safer around children and pets.) In terms of style, the more casual the room, the more one is inclined to choose blinds or shutters for its window dressing.

Within the wide world of blinds and shutters, your choice should be guided by the style and material that best complement other elements in the room as well as by your goals for light and privacy (information in the adjacent box and on the opposite page will help you evaluate your options). Fabric may be preferred, to soften a room or to co-ordinate with other furnishings; use Venetian blinds or shutters to add architectural interest to a plain space. Natural woven window treatments – grasses, reeds, matchstick, and bamboo – are suitable even in dressy settings and instantly bring contrast to any room. They contribute texture both through their materials and with the light patterns they create. Panel track blinds, available in a variety of fabrics and materials, are a sleek new style that offer privacy and effectively block sunlight.

Roman Blinds

Tailored treatments that pull up in flat folds, Roman blinds can be fitted inside or outside the window frame. They work well with a variety of fabrics, from sheer linen to heavyweight canvas.

Roller Blinds

The simplest type of retractable opaque blinds, fabric roller blinds can be found ready-made in basic colours or can be custom ordered to match your wall colour or upholstery.

Bottom-Up Blinds

A popular design for urban living, these ensure privacy while admitting light through the upper portion. They're available in bottom-mounted roller designs and also in custom materials.

Honeycomb Blinds

Honeycomb and pleated blinds, made from materials and fabrics designed to hold their pleats permanently, are softer than standard blinds and admit light through their translucent materials.

Venetian Blinds

This classic style remains popular due to its versatility. Venetian blinds provide privacy and excellent light control, and cast attractive patterns of sunlight and shadow.

Vertical Blinds

Similar to panel track blinds, vertical vanes 8 cm (3 ½ in) wide slide on a track and stack to one side. They're a good solution for large windows and sliding doors and are available in various lengths.

Track Panels

Useful for windows or sliding glass doors, these vertical panels 20–45 cm (8–18 in) wide, made of fabric or natural woven material, slide on a track and stack to one side when open.

Louvred Shutters

Slatted shutters can be adjusted to admit as much light as desired, though they do not close tightly enough to block light out completely. Made of wood or synthetics, they can be stained or painted.

Panelled Shutters

Solid wooden shutters are a smart choice in cities, where street noise is an issue; in cold climates, where they provide insulation; and in children's bedrooms, where they block out light and sound.

Asymmetrical Elegance, *left*
Even formal window treatments like this velvet and embroidered voile pairing take on a more offhand air when given an unexpected, asymmetrical treatment. Here, two velvet panels are pulled to one side and tied back with a pepperberry spray. A single panel of embroidered voile on the back rod is pulled neatly across the window to filter incoming daylight.

Simple and Striking, *right*
If you have a light and airy room and want to preserve that sense of openness, Roman blinds are a great option. They offer a polished look and effective light control, but keep a window looking neat and leave window mouldings and walls unadorned. Roman blinds are available in a wide array of materials and fabrics, either ready-made or customized to match upholstery or wall colour. Here, bold stripes make a strong statement and add punch to a white room.

The way that we perceive a room – as restful, romantic, welcoming, or cold – depends very much on how it is lit. It's helpful to understand the three main types of lighting – ambient, task, and accent – so that you can use them to best effect. Ambient light is generally the available natural light during the day; at night it's usually provided by a central overhead fixture, lamps, or a group of recessed lights that evenly illuminate an entire room. Task lighting is self-explanatory, directing light for

WORKING WITH
LIGHTING

LAMPLIGHT EXTENDS OUR DAYS, AIDS OUR EYESIGHT, AND INFLUENCES OUR MOODS. NO SINGLE SOURCE WORKS ON ITS OWN, SO PLAN FOR A DIVERSE, BALANCED MIX.

specific activities. Accent lights are the jewellery of a room – the spots, candles, and picture lights that add sparkle. But all lighting fixtures can add to a room's style. A reading lamp with an opaque shade throws strong light onto the table top, calling attention to a featured object and serving as accent as well as task lighting. Recessed ceiling fixtures can be fitted with wall-washer bulbs or with spots that call attention to an architectural feature, a work of art, or a whole bookcase. A small chandelier can deliver part of a room's ambient light while serving as a dramatic focal point. Use function and style together to achieve the best effect.

Day to Night

Light is never constant. It shifts by the second, transforming an interior space, and our moods along with it. Celebrate the evening by orchestrating your own effects.

A bright, open space by day can seem a more intimate and secluded spot by night with the simple flip of a switch. It's human nature to be drawn to light as the sky darkens and rooms grow dimmer with the setting sun. In colder seasons we gather around the fireplace for both light and warmth. But summer months benefit from flickering flames as well, in the form of candles, which also draw guests together. Make the most of a seating group already arranged around a fireplace and add votives on the cocktail table, or dramatize the moment with a collection of grand tapers in assorted candlesticks on the mantel. Candlelight and firelight are known as "kinetic light", which has special appeal because of its movement. Supplement its enchanting attraction with low levels of ambient lighting, to create a more comfortable light balance within the room and prevent potential mishaps as people move around.

This **open-plan room**, *right and opposite page,* is lit by a skylight and floor-to-ceiling windows by day. At night, a floor lamp and a recessed spotlight on the mantel provide illumination; votive candles reflected on lustrous surfaces set a festive mood.

DESIGN LESSON THE COLOUR OF LIGHT

Understanding that different kinds of lightbulbs emit slightly different colours of light is critical to planning flattering lighting for your home. Lamps that give off a warmer colour enhance skin tones, putting you and your guests in a better light. Whiter light is better for task work like reading and for illuminating artwork. Full-spectrum light is most like natural light and is quite versatile. Painted walls are especially affected by lighting's colour, so it's important to evaluate sample wall colours in artificial light, particularly for dining rooms and bedrooms, which are so often used at night.

■ INCANDESCENT LIGHT is warm and flatters the skin. Easily controlled by dimmers or with three-way bulbs, it is versatile enough to be used for ambient, task, or accent lighting.

■ HALOGEN BULBS produce the whitest light of any bulb and thus do not influence the colour of furnishings or art. They're considered the best choice for task lighting.

■ FLUORESCENT LIGHT, which had a bad name in the past, is now often colour-corrected to simulate daylight. The most energy-efficient of all lamps, fluorescent lights are available as tubes as well as screw-in and bayonet bulbs.

Lamps

The role of lamps in balancing the lighting of any room is critical because they offer the ultimate flexibility to supplement built-in fixtures.

The most comfortable rooms are those that evenly balance light from diverse sources. Ideally, light sources within one room sit at different levels. Ambient lighting tends to come from the ceiling; table and floor lamps bring spots of light into the centre of the space, helping to disperse light throughout the room; accent lights are most often directed towards a wall, a mantel, or another architectural feature, or are focussed on a painting or sculptural object. A lampshade is also an influence on a harmonious lighting plan. An opaque or semi-opaque shade is not only a stylish choice but is also recommended for reading because it focusses light onto a page. Lamps arranged around a conversation seating area may cast a more diffuse light and so should be dressed accordingly. Translucent vellum shades give off a soft golden glow; silk shades lined with fabric cast an especially gentle and flattering light and create a sense of intimacy in a room.

Within the same space, lamps need not match but should be of compatible styles. Choosing shades in a single palette will unify a grouping of different lamps. If you'd like to feature one unique decorative lamp and give it focus, choose more understated styles for other lamps in the room, such as an office-style lamp, which seems almost to disappear. Sometimes a shaded lamp that sits in the centre of a room can be a visual barrier, whereas a slim-profile lamp will tend to open up a space.

An opaque shade, *left*, turns a decorative task lamp into an accent light, casting directional light that illuminates table accessories.

Work Light

An adjustable-arm work lamp is a longtime favourite that allows you to direct light just where you want it. The ideal height puts the bottom of the lampshade at eye-level or just below. See other desk lamp options below.

Bedside Lamp

Recommended height for a bedside lamp is 51 cm (20 in) from your pillow to the bottom of the shade. A relatively opaque shade helps concentrate light on the page. See more options for bedside lighting below.

Floor Lamp

Light from a floor lamp should fall unobstructed over your shoulder. For lamps at the side of a chair, the distance from floor to bottom of shade should be 102–107 cm (40–42 in), or at about eye-level. See another chairside option below.

Vintage-Style Desk Lamp

A crook-arm–style lamp with a metal shade makes a stylish alternative to an adjustable lamp on a small desk, but it has a more limited range of illumination and therefore requires especially good ambient light to accompany it.

Swing-Arm Wall Fixture

A popular alternative to the table lamp, the swing-arm lamp offers greater flexibility in positioning the light for reading and frees up space on the bedside table. Most swing-arm fixtures are mains-wired and so must be custom fit.

Table Lamp

The bottom of a table lamp's shade should be about 38 cm (15 in) above the desk surface for optimal reading light. A translucent shade helps eliminate glare and contributes to a room's ambient light while still serving as task lighting.

Adjustable-Arm Clip-On Lamp

An adjustable clip-on lamp makes an economic and stylish bedside lamp when attached to a headboard or a bedside table. You can control both its horizontal and vertical position and the span of light that it casts.

Swing-Arm Office-Style Lamp

An adjustable lamp allows family members to position the light exactly at their eye-levels for reading. Its slim profile makes it unobtrusive. Aim the bowl towards a wall or turn it up to the ceiling for ambient lighting.

A Balanced Mix, *left*

Gradations of light give a room greater depth. Multiple sources of light are well balanced here, from the hanging drum shades to votive candles clustered on the table and pillar candles on the mantel. As night falls and guests gather, the effect becomes more dramatic. Light draws attention wherever it is placed or focussed, so keep a room visually lively with thoughtful placement of sources and gleaming surfaces to catch and reflect it.

Warm and Welcoming, *right*

Electric- and candlelight combine to give this tailored living room a welcoming atmosphere. The translucent shade of a floor lamp casts a warm glow while the opaque shade on the wall sconce focusses light on the wall and mantel below. A white vase in the mantel grouping holds a votive candle in a nice counterpoint to the sconce; tapers on the coffee table bring a glow to the centre of the room.

Multi-use Versatility, *left*

This combination family room–home office space benefits from a well-designed lighting plan. Dimmable halogen wall fixtures can be turned upwards to provide an ambient wash or downwards to focus on the photographs and illuminate the desk and sofa. The articulated desk lamp can be adjusted for users at the sofa or worktable. Both demonstrate how task lighting also contributes to a room's ambient lighting.

MATERIALS

kona solid hardwood flooring

laminate flooring in walnut

engineered flooring in stained oak

bamboo flooring

Guide to Materials

Whether you are redecorating your entire home or simply sprucing up a room, choosing materials is a key step in the process. The right materials achieve the look you want, prove practical for your uses, and meet your budget requirements.

Flooring

Solid wood flooring *(pictured above)* is available in a variety of species, from traditional English oak to beech and salvaged pine. Prices vary considerably, with domestic and European species at the low end of the price ladder and less abundant exotics at the top. Wood can be stained to just about any colour, and it can be re-sanded and refinished when it begins to look worn. Lighter woods lend themselves to casual decorating styles, while darker woods, such as walnut or wenge, suggest more formal interiors. Strip flooring comes in a few standard widths, starting at 6 cm (2 ¼ in). Planks of pine, walnut, and other wood species up to 51 cm (20 in) wide also are available (expect to pay a premium for those). Flooring can be finished on-site, or at the factory before installation (see Flooring Finishes for Wood, page 358).

Laminate flooring *(pictured above)* is made to look like wood flooring, but it's actually a high-tech marriage of MDF and a thin, photo-like layer protected by a clear plastic film. It is often used in mudrooms and hallways or in commercial applications. Less expensive than conventional wood flooring, laminate flooring is made by a number of companies and is easy to find at DIY stores. You can install laminate flooring yourself without hiring a professional. Newer versions come in a number of wood tones and have guarantees of up to 25 years. Unlike wood, a laminate floor can't be refinished.

Engineered flooring *(pictured above)* is made from several thin sheets of wood that are glued together to make a plank. It works in places that solid wood flooring can't, such as a basement, where it can be placed directly over concrete. The top layer can be a different wood species from the rest of the plank, allowing manufacturers to offer a range of woods. Most engineered flooring comes already finished, and some brands have a thick enough top layer to be re-sanded just like solid wood flooring. Another advantage: planks come in widths up to 18 cm (7 in). The best grades are comparable in cost to conventional solid wood. Brand names include Meister, Bruce, Kährs, Nätura, and Karelia.

Bamboo flooring *(pictured above)* is quickly gaining popularity for its light, natural colouring and attractive texture. Bamboo flooring also makes environmental sense because it's made from a fast-growing plant that's ready to harvest in as little as four years. After harvesting, bamboo stalks are cut into strips and then laminated into pieces of flooring as durable as oak. Bamboo can be ordered unfinished or factory finished. Because it doesn't shrink and expand as much as solid wood flooring, it's a good choice over under-floor heating systems. Bamboo can be used in any room of the house, but take care in a bathroom or other wet areas: like solid wood flooring, bamboo can be damaged by water.

Rubber flooring is more often seen in commercial or industrial settings, but it's also an option where its durability and resilience underfoot make it a practical choice, such as in a kitchen, home gym, or playroom. Rubber flooring is available in sheet and tile forms. Varieties with surface textures have more slip resistance than plain flooring and are often specified for contemporary kitchens because they're both stylish and easy on the feet. Selection is somewhat limited. Rubber flooring is comparable in cost to good-quality vinyl, and less expensive than solid or engineered wood flooring and many types of ceramic and stone tile.

Cork flooring is enjoying a resurgence of interest, in part because it's a natural product made from a renewable resource and because modern finishes have made maintenance easier. Available in tile or plank form, cork is a resilient floor that's warm and comfortable underfoot. Cork should be sealed after installation, and the finish will need periodic maintenance. It's available in several densities, with higher densities contributing to longer wear. Like wood, cork expands and contracts with moisture, so it's not the best choice for a bathroom or utility room. When used in the kitchen, high-wear work areas should be protected with rugs. Cork is comparable in cost to moderately priced wood.

Linoleum flooring is an old-fashioned favourite made from renewable resources including wood flour, linseed oil, and ground limestone. Durable, resilient, and comfortable underfoot, it's available in many colours and patterns, in sheet form as well as tiles. Although vinyl largely displaced linoleum because it didn't need as much maintenance, newer versions of linoleum do not require waxing. Linoleum costs more than most vinyl and should be installed professionally.

Vinyl remains a popular resilient flooring, in part because it needs very little maintenance. The patterns on inlaid vinyl go all the way through the material so they don't wear off. More expensive versions have a top surface, called the wear layer, made with extremely tough materials like aluminium oxide to withstand heavy foot traffic. Prices vary considerably, but economical varieties are among the least expensive flooring options available.

Natural stone tiles are available in many materials, including limestone, slate, soapstone, marble, and granite. Stone makes a durable, naturally beautiful flooring material that doesn't need much maintenance. Because of its density, stone is a good choice over under-floor heating systems, and it stays cool underfoot in warm weather. All stone, with the exception of soapstone, should be sealed

cast-earth flooring

undermount sink

pedestal sink

belfast sink

to prevent staining and may require periodic re-sealing. Stone tiles, like ceramic tiles, shouldn't be installed over a bouncy subfloor, so existing floors may need reinforcing if you're thinking of re-flooring with tiles. Stone flooring typically costs more than ceramic tiles, and it can be quite expensive.

Ceramic tiles are available in many colours, textures, and sizes – from small mosaics to pieces up to 45 cm (18 in) square – making them an attractive and less costly alternative to natural stone. Glazed ceramic tiles require no sealing and no maintenance beyond regular sweeping and washing. Textured surfaces and unglazed tiles are not as slippery as smooth, glazed surfaces. For wet areas like the bathroom, look for tiles with slip resistance. Tiles absorb heat, so they're a good choice over under-floor heating systems.

Handmade clay paving stones in characteristic earth tones, such as the clay Saltillo tiles made in Mexico, are typically air-dried and then fired at low temperatures. They have pleasing variations in thickness, flatness, and colouration. Because they are porous, these paving stones should be sealed and are not considered suitable for wet locations. Cast-earth flooring tiles (pictured above) are created by pouring a mixture of earth, water, and cement into moulds to make a highly insulating material.

Concrete, long used for garage and basement floors, is enjoying new popularity as a finish floor in the rest of the house. It's just as hard-wearing as ceramic tiles and can be treated with stains and colourants to produce a range of surface appearances that may surprise

you. Concrete is a naturally porous material that must be sealed to resist stains, but it also can be enlivened with a variety of decorative inlays – metal, wood, even seashells. Like tile and stone floor surfaces, concrete is a natural fit with under-floor heat. But it's also heavy, something to take into account when planning. Concrete floors vary quite a bit in cost, depending on how the surface is finished, but they are typically less expensive than stone.

Bricks make an extremely durable, colourfast floor surface. Thin clay bricks designed especially for interior flooring are installed like ceramic tiles and are available in more than a dozen colours. Their surface texture gives them good slip resistance, and they can be set in a variety of decorative patterns. Brick tiles vary in size, so a fairly wide grout joint may be recommended. Sealing bricks makes them easier to maintain. Prices are comparable to many kinds of ceramic tiles.

Flooring Finishes for Wood

Oil-modified polyurethane is a tough, long-wearing floor finish whose ingredients impart a characteristic amber colour to wood flooring. It's especially noticeable on floors made of lighter woods. Oil-based finishes generally cost less than water-based finishes, but they take longer to dry, and the volatile organic compounds (VOCs) they contain give off an odour as they cure. The good news is that it takes fewer coats of finish to complete the job.

Water-based urethane floor finishes are water clear, so they don't give wood the same amber cast that oil-based finishes do. They dry faster than oil-modified

urethanes, and they don't give off the same odour. For all of these reasons, water-based finishes are becoming more widely used, even if they are trickier to apply. On the downside, they typically cost more and it may take more coats to get the same level of protection.

Pre-finished flooring gets a protective coating at the factory, so you don't have to sand, seal, or apply a protective finish after flooring is installed. Factory finishes are applied to many brands of wood and engineered wood flooring. Formulations may contain tough ceramic particles for long wear – and long warranties.

Kitchen/Bathroom Sinks

Types of Sinks

Sinks for kitchens and bathrooms are no longer a design afterthought. New shapes, materials, and colours allow hardworking sinks to make a style statement. There are three key factors in choosing a sink: what it's made from, how big it is, and how it will be installed. For the kitchen, there are many different sink sizes available, from the two-bowl design that fits in a 90 cm- (36 in-) wide sink cupboard to models with extra-deep 28 cm (11 in) bowls, which make washing big pots and pans much easier.

Undermount sinks (pictured above) leave an easy-to-clean, uninterrupted work surface because there's no sink rim to collect debris. Undermounts work best with worktops made from a solid material, such as stone or concrete, but don't lend themselves to plastic-laminate worktops because the sink cut-out leaves edges of the worktop substrate exposed.

Surface-mounted sinks sit on the worktop, so they can be used with any kind of worktop material. Because the sink's rim can trap food and water, it's not as easy to keep clean as an undermount sink.

Flush-mounted sinks are much like surface-mounted sinks except that the lip of the sink is designed to sit flush with a surrounding tile worktop. They have the same advantages of an undermount sink because there's no lip at the edge of the sink to catch crumbs or water. Like surface-mounted sinks, they should be sealed to the worktop to prevent leaks.

Integral sinks are part of the worktop itself. They can be fabricated from solid surface material (such as DuPont's Corian) and glued into the worktop, or made from stainless steel and welded into a stainless steel worktop – just like you'd find in a commercial kitchen.

Pedestal sinks (pictured above), a bathroom classic, take up less room than a conventional sink and vanity, an advantage in a small bathroom. They don't provide as much storage space, but a narrow shelf over the sink can help. Most if not all pedestal sinks are vitreous china, made by firing glazed clay at a high temperature to produce a nonporous surface.

Belfast sinks (pictured above) are traditionally made of porcelain over cast iron but they are also available in other materials such as stone and fire clay. What they have in common is a broad front face that is left exposed by special sink cupboards. The look has a pleasing vintage flavour to it, not unlike the shallow slate sinks that once were common in farm-houses. Belfast sinks are a good match for casual, country-style kitchens.

stainless steel worktop

granite worktop

limestone worktop

maple butcher's-block worktop

Sink Materials

Stainless steel is the most popular material for kitchen sinks. It has a number of advantages: it won't absorb food or bacteria, doesn't rust, is unaffected by heat, and is relatively easy to clean. Basic stainless steel sinks are made from 20- or 22-gauge metal; better grades are made from 18-gauge or even 16-gauge steel. Brushed and polished finishes are available. Prices vary considerably.

Fire-clay, or vitreous china, sinks are made from a durable, high-temperature ceramic material. They are the same all the way through, so a chip won't uncover an underlying layer of metal that can rust. Their smooth surfaces may look something like porcelain, but fire-clay sinks can be finely detailed with surface decoration or paint before they are fired, giving them unique decorative characteristics. Basic fire-clay sinks are competitive in cost with other types, although elaborately detailed models can be quite expensive.

Porcelain over cast iron is a time-tested combination that many of us may remember from our grandmother's kitchen. With proper care, the porcelain top surface is very durable but can be damaged by abrasive cleaners. The cast-iron core has good thermal retention once it's been warmed up, and the mass of these sinks makes them quiet when water is running or when they're equipped with a waste disposer. Basic two-bowl models are relatively low in cost. Enamelled steel sinks are a lighter, less expensive option, but they are known to chip more easily than porcelain sinks.

Copper and bronze sinks are among the most expensive sink options, but these non-corroding metals are very durable and have an appealing rustic character. Copper, the less expensive of the two, needs regular cleaning to look its best. Bronze develops a darker surface patina.

Vessel sinks in the bathroom may remind you of an old-fashioned wash basin set on top of a chest of drawers. Many are designed to sit on top of a vanity unit, but wall-mounted models are also available. There are many materials to choose from, including tempered glass, ceramic, copper, bronze, and stone. Vessel sinks can become a design focal point in a bathroom. Because the walls of the sink rise above the worktop, one consideration is the height of the vanity unit on which it sits. A higher sink may make life a little easier for anyone who hates to stoop over a conventional sink, but not as convenient for children. Vessel sinks may be fitted with wall-mounted or extra-tall taps.

Kitchen Worktops

Plastic laminate is an economical worktop choice available in a huge variety of colours and patterns. It's not as heat resistant as other materials and will be damaged by sharp knives, but it's a long-wearing material that requires practically no maintenance and is easy to keep clean. Laminate can be bought in sheet form and installed over a chipboard substrate, or bought as a "post-formed" worktop with an integral backsplash and a rolled front edge that's ready for installation. One common objection to laminate is a dark line where

the top meets the outside edge, but there are several ways of avoiding it. One is to use a type of laminate that has solid colour throughout. Another is to ask the installer to add wood or bevelled laminate edgings, which completely disguise the seam.

Stainless steel and other metals can be fashioned into very durable, heat-resistant worktops. Stainless steel *(pictured above)* is non-absorptive and easy to keep clean (one reason it's the standard in commercial kitchens), and a worktop can be made with an integral sink of the same material. Thicker sheets are better at resisting dents. Stainless steel can be scratched, but in time these minor imperfections blend together to create a pleasing patina. Stainless steel is a moderately expensive worktop choice.

Ceramic tile worktops, just like tile floors, are highly resistant to wear, and the tremendous variety in tile colours, patterns, and textures opens the door to virtually unlimited design possibilities. Ceramic tiles are heat resistant and fairly easy to install. A tile worktop, however, is hard and unforgiving, and grout lines make the surface somewhat irregular. The result is that glasses tip easily and are more likely to break on the hard tiles. A tile surface is extremely durable, but if a tile should become damaged it can be replaced without tearing out the whole worktop. Prices vary based on the type of tile.

Natural stone worktops can be installed as a slab or as individual tiles. Stone comes in a beautiful array of colours, from dark-flecked granite *(pictured above)* and grey soapstone to white marble and pale,

mottled limestone *(pictured above)*. Overall, stone is extremely durable and resistant to heat, but like tiles it can be tough on delicate glassware. Most stone should be treated with a sealer to prevent stains (soapstone is an exception). Limestone and some light-coloured marbles will not keep their pristine surface, even after sealing, and may stain over time. If possible, try to see a stone worktop that's been in place for a few years and compare it with what you see in the showroom. Stone is a relatively expensive option.

Wood has been supplanted as a worktop material in many homes by a host of newer materials that require less maintenance. Yet it remains a naturally warm and attractive material that can be protected from water with a sealer. Butcher's block made from maple *(pictured above)* is a frequent choice, but worktops are fashioned from just about any kind of wood. Prices vary with the type of wood, but it can be an economical option.

Solid-surface worktops are practical: easy to clean, easy to repair, and available in many colours and patterns. They can also be combined with an integral sink of the same material. More gentle on plates and glasses than either stone or tile, they also don't stain easily, if at all. Known widely as Corian (which is made by DuPont), solid surfaces are also manufactured by a number of other companies. These worktops are moderately expensive.

Concrete is currently a popular choice for worktops. Because it can be formed into virtually any shape or thickness and enlivened with almost any kind of inlay,

framed face cupboards

frameless face cupboards

laminate cupboards

cherry wood cupboards

concrete offers unrivalled design possibilities. It can be cast in place or in a workshop and then installed like a stone slab. Like tile and stone, concrete is an unforgiving surface and will absorb stains if left unsealed. Concrete tends to be a relatively expensive installation.

Stone composites, such as Silestone and Zodiaq, are blends of mostly real stone and a resin binder along with pigments for colour. They are more uniform and predictable than natural stone and slightly less expensive. Quartz composites are very tough and, unlike real stone, won't absorb stains. Stone composite worktops are easy to maintain.

Kitchen and Bathroom Cupboards

Types of Cupboards

Kitchen and bathroom cupboards are available in just about any architectural style and price range. Whether you're looking for a distressed antique finish, easy-to-clean laminate, or natural wood, you should be able to find just what you want. The most economical cupboard lines – what the cupboard industry calls "stock" – have the most limited choices in finish, materials, and hardware. Semi-custom-built cupboards offer more diverse finishes as well as superior materials and construction (dovetailed solid wooden drawers, for example, rather than hardboard). Both stock and semi-custom lines are built in approximate increments of 7.5 cm (3 in), so filler strips are used to fit them to a room that doesn't fall exactly on that grid. At the top end are fully

custom-built cupboards, made to any size and with virtually any material. Because custom-built cupboards are made to order, be prepared to wait to get them, and prices can be steep.

Framed face cupboards *(pictured above)* are traditional in appearance, thanks to a wooden frame applied to the face of the cupboard box that creates openings for drawers and doors. Depending on the look you want, framed face cupboards can be ordered with inset or overlay doors and drawers, and with exposed or hidden door hardware. Cupboards can be ordered in many natural woods, including oak and maple, with a variety of stains, or with painted or glazed surfaces.

Frameless face cupboards *(pictured above)*, a construction technique that originated in post-war Europe, are more contemporary in appearance than framed face cupboards. Doors and drawer fronts cover the front of cupboard boxes completely, so all you see are the narrow gaps between doors and drawers. Frameless face cupboards have a little more room inside because there's no overhanging face frame, and changing the entire look of the kitchen is as simple as buying new doors and drawer fronts.

Cupboard Materials

Melamine is one of the most economical materials available for cupboard construction. It consists of chipboard topped by a thin layer of plastic resin. High-pressure laminate *(pictured above)*, the same material that's used to make kitchen worktops, is also used as a finish material in cupboard construction. Of the two, laminate is more durable, but both are

available in many colours and are easy to keep clean because they won't absorb spills. One disadvantage, especially with melamine, is that the surface is difficult to repair if it chips. On laminate doors, the dark lines along seams and edges can be concealed with PVC tape or by using colour-through laminate.

Thermofoil doors and drawers are made to look like painted wood, but they are actually plastic that's formed around a core of MDF. Because the MDF takes such crisp detailing, you can get the look of a traditional raised panel door or drawer in an easy-care material and at a lower cost. A thermofoil door doesn't have as many seams as one made from high-pressure laminate, which means fewer places where seams could separate, but thermofoil isn't as heat tolerant.

Wooden cupboards have a warmth and character that no manmade material can duplicate completely. Hardwoods and veneers such as oak, maple, cherry *(pictured above)*, and alder are available from many manufacturers and make durable, handsome cupboards. If your style is a little less traditional, there are many other species to choose from – Douglas fir, quarter-sawn white oak, antique heart pine, and mahogany, for example. Keep in mind, that the more exotic the wood, the more it will cost.

Finishes for natural wooden cupboards run the gamut, from crystal clear varnish to colour-tinted lacquer and sophisticated marriages of glaze and stain. While wood can be stained to just about any shade, you can also rely more on wood's natural appearance by working from a basic

palette of textures and colours – think blond maple versus a dark ruby cherry. In addition to offering clear-coat finishes, manufacturers in recent years have broadened their offerings of glazes. These more complex surfaces include a second colour layer that is applied and then mostly, but not completely, wiped away. The process leaves vestiges of colour in corners and along moulding profiles. If you like the look of age, choose cupboards whose finishes have been intentionally distressed or sanded through at the factory. These finishes mimic the effects of years of use, exactly the right effect in a renovated country kitchen.

Redecorating Cupboards

Paint applied by brush or spray gun is a simple way of coaxing new life out of old kitchen cabinets without much expense, as long as the cupboards are structurally sound. Finishes won't be quite as durable as those applied in the factory to new cupboards, so expect to touch up chips and nicks periodically (make sure the painter leaves some paint behind). Replacing hardware at the same time completes the make-over.

Re-facing cupboards with wood and adding new drawer fronts and doors is another way of reviving a tired kitchen. It's almost always less expensive than tearing out old cupboards and replacing them, and the process usually takes only a few days. Lots of wood species are available. Specialized craftsmen make doors and drawer fronts in their workshops, and veneer components like cupboard boxes right in your kitchen. New hardware completes the transformation.

claw-foot bathtub

bathtub with concrete surround and tap

glass-door ceramic tile shower

glass mosaic tile shower

Bathtubs

Porcelain enamel over cast iron makes an extremely durable bathtub. Claw-foot bathtubs *(pictured above)* have a vintage look that's prized today. They are available new, and old ones can still be found in salvage yards, proof of just how long they hold up. These bathtubs get their long life from the process by which they're made: an enamel mixture is sprayed onto a moulded cast-iron core and the bathtub is fired at a high temperature, fusing the two materials and creating a stain-resistant, easy-to-clean surface. Be careful not to use abrasive cleaners, which can damage the surface. Cast-iron bathtubs are good at retaining heat for a long soak.

Enamelled steel is a low-cost alternative to porcelain enamel over cast iron. These bathtubs are also lighter in weight, so they won't dampen the sound of running water or hold heat quite as effectively as cast iron. Although economy steel bathtubs are not as durable as cast iron, some higher-priced versions combine alloy steel with a structural composite underneath for longer life and better insulation.

Fibreglass bathtubs, among the most economical options, are made by spraying a smooth resin coating on a mould and reinforcing the back with fibreglass and resin. The thin outer layer of a fibreglass bath is not as durable as other materials, and the finish can be damaged by careless cleaning. Still, a fibreglass bathtub may be a good choice in a bathroom that isn't used every day, like a holiday home or guest bathroom.

Acrylic bathtubs are more durable and scratch resistant than polyester bathtubs, and come with a proportionally higher price. The outer colour layer is thicker, which helps the bathtub last longer. Like fibreglass bathtubs, the shells of acrylic bathtubs are reinforced with another material for strength.

Replacement bathtub liners made from acrylic plastic can save the trouble and expense of tearing out and replacing a bathtub that's seen better days. After taking measurements and ordering components, a contractor returns to install the new liner and shower walls in about a day. Although the process is not inexpensive, it's less costly than employing a plumber, buying a new bathtub, and waiting for the work to be finished.

Old bathtubs stained and chipped from decades of use can be refinished on-site. Technicians thoroughly clean the surface, fill chips and scratches, and apply a new topcoat. A sprayed acrylic, which takes about a day to cure, can have either a matt or gloss finish. Many specialized contractors offer the service. Pristine white again, the acrylic surface will have a plastic quality that the original enamel didn't. Try to see samples of the coating or a refinished bath before you commit.

Speciality Bathtubs

Soaking bathtubs are a long-standing tradition in Japan that for good reason is gaining popularity worldwide. Few things are as thoroughly relaxing as sitting in hot, chin-deep water at the end of the day. Ranging from 51 cm (20 in) to as deep as 90 cm (36 in), soaking bathtubs are much deeper than standard bathtubs and are a big part of the trend toward free-standing bathtubs in today's bathrooms. Extra-tall soaking bathtubs can be hard to get into; you may need a wide, sturdy stepstool to help. Something else to keep in mind: as bathtubs get deeper and hold more water, their weight increases. An 81 cm- (32 in-) deep bathtub may hold 227–284 litres (50–62 gallons) of water, a potential strain on floor framing as well as a standard-capacity hot-water heater.

Whirlpool bathtubs add jets of water to the bath for an aquatic massage that can be adjusted in intensity. Whirlpools are considerably more expensive than standard bathtubs, but they ease tired muscles at the end of a long day, and some can accommodate more than one person. Very large bathtubs hold 568 litres (150 gallons) or more of water and may require special floor framing for support as well as dedicated hot-water equipment.

Air-jet bathtubs use streams of bubbles instead of jets of water to relax the bather. Because they don't recirculate water through an internal network of pipes, they require less maintenance than a whirlpool. They are also somewhat less expensive than the most elaborate whirlpools.

Showers

Custom-tiled showers *(pictured above)* provide unrivalled design possibilities. Shower trays made on-site with a mortar bed can be constructed in any size and shape, and a truly vast selection of ceramic and stone tiles offers colours, textures, and patterns to suit any taste. Tiled showers can be designed so they don't need a door, and they may be sunlit by glass-block windows or walls. Many kinds of ceramic and stone tiles can be used, but stay away from smooth, highly polished surfaces on the floor, as they can be slippery. Shower tiles can be specified in smaller sizes to prevent slipping.

One-piece bathtub/shower combination units are available in fibreglass or acrylic. Fully enclosed acrylic bathtub/showers with integral ceilings can be fitted with steam generators or elaborate multihead showers. Because of their size, one-piece bathtub/showers may not fit through halls and doorways during renovation work, but manufacturers also offer two- and three-piece models that can be negotiated into a bathroom more easily.

Self-contained shower cubicles fit in smaller spaces than a combination bathtub/shower. There is a considerable range of designs and cost, including acrylic and fibreglass models that fit snugly into a corner and those with curved or angled faces. Larger units may include features such as moulded seats, adjustable showerheads, and built-in wall niches.

Toilets

Toilets come in a variety of styles and price ranges, but by government regulation they are now required to use no more than 6 litres (1.3 gallons) of water per flush – a far cry from the 11–19 litres (2.4–4.2 gallons) that older toilets typically used. Floor-mounted toilets are the most common type, but wall-mounted models also are available. They free up more floor space, making the bathroom look bigger, and they also make cleaning more convenient. Taller-than-average models better accommodate the needs of someone who uses a wheelchair or who has trouble sitting down and standing up.

teak

painted wicker

powder-coated aluminium

cotton matelassé

There are two basic toilet designs. By far the most common are the gravity-feed designs. They release the contents of a cistern when the flush valve is opened and rely on gravity and the weight of water to do the rest. In the US, pressure-assist toilets tap the pressure in the plumbing system or use a pump to help expel waste. In some models, water consumption is less than the 6 litre- (1.6-gallon-) standard. Power-assist models provide a forceful flushing action, but they're typically more expensive and noisier.

Two-piece toilets consist of a bowl and a separate cistern that are connected by the plumber at the time of installation. Some models are specially designed for corner installations. Old-fashioned toilets with the cistern mounted high on the wall are still available.

Close-coupled toilets, which tend to be more expensive, have fewer crevices and seams than two-piece designs. They look more contemporary and are easier to clean.

Outdoor Furniture

Teak *(pictured above)* is the benchmark for outdoor wooden furniture: beautiful, long-lasting, and virtually maintenance-free. The luxuriant brown colour of this tropical hardwood fades to a silver-grey over time, yet the oil-rich wood needs only an occasional scrubbing to maintain its subdued good looks.

Mahogany is a long-standing favourite, in part because of the wood's high rot resistance and its deep reddish-brown colour. Long a favourite of boatbuilders, mahogany was the material used in

the original deck chairs on the *Titanic* (a Nantucket, Massachusetts, company produces a line of reproduction deck chairs based on one salvaged at the scene of the 1912 North Atlantic wreck). The wood weathers naturally to a soft grey.

A variety of tropical hardwoods, such as ipé, jarrah, balau, and nyatoh, are alternatives to the better-known teak and mahogany. Prices should be less than what you'd pay for top grades of teak, but these woods also are strong, dense, and weather resistant. Reddish-brown colours fade to an attractive silver-grey with exposure to sun and rain, but an application of oil can restore the original colour.

Cedar and redwood are alternatives to imported tropical hardwoods. Both of these North American softwoods have long histories as durable outdoor building materials with excellent resistance to rot and insects. Clear, tight-grained heartwood promises the best weather resistance, but supplies are dwindling. Neither of these woods is as dense as the tropical hardwoods, making them a little more susceptible to wear and tear. And unlike the tropicals, they need periodic applications of wood preservative.

Wicker furniture *(pictured above)* is generally woven from flexible branches or twigs. Synthetic fibres are now being used to create wicker for all-weather outdoor use. Unlike natural wicker furniture, all-season versions are woven over frames of aluminium or plastic and can be left out in the rain, even snow, with little or no ill effect. Best of all, they have all the comfort and charm of the real thing.

Rattan, water hyacinth, seagrass, and abaca are all plant fibres used to make

attractive woven furniture with a natural outdoors look. These fibres can be dyed, but they're not intended to be left outside. Count on protecting them from sun and rain under a patio or veranda roof.

Cast iron and wrought iron are timeless choices for patio and garden furniture, and they won't get blown around in a storm. Metal can be formed into just about any shape, opening the door to ornate designs that aren't possible with other materials. Iron rusts when exposed to water, so it must be painted (and repainted periodically) to protect it. Alternately, some manufacturers apply a plastic-like coating to ward off corrosion.

Aluminium is the most widely used material for outdoor furniture today, and it has one big advantage over iron: it won't rust. But, left unprotected, aluminium will pit and oxidize in the weather, so look for furniture that has a protective powder-coated finish *(pictured above)*. Outdoor aluminium furniture comes in a variety of grades. Hollow tubular furniture is the most economical choice and offers lightweight portability. Furniture made from cast aluminium components is heavier, sturdier, and available in many styles and finishes, though top grades can be quite expensive.

Plastic is an inexpensive and durable material that can be moulded into a variety of shapes for outdoor furniture. Armed with UV inhibitors, plastic is impervious to the weather and available in bright colours. If you're looking for the benefits of plastic in traditional styles, there's now furniture made from recycled plastic that looks like painted wood. Adirondack-style and rocking chairs are among the offerings.

Weather-resistant cushions and fabrics add a burst of colour and texture to metal and wooden furniture, and make a long Sunday afternoon lounge a lot more comfortable. Plain cotton canvas that had to be raced inside during a rainstorm has given way to much hardier synthetic materials that look great, resist fading, and are easier to clean. Weather-treated canvas is also available.

Fabrics

Canvas is a heavy-duty fabric commonly used to make sporting goods, awnings, and tents. Woven from cotton, linen, or hemp, canvas has a casual, relaxed appearance and can be used inside or out for upholstery and cushions. It's an excellent choice for outdoor furniture cushions; look for canvas that has been treated with Teflon to repel water and resist sun fading.

Chenille weaves silk, cotton, or synthetic fibres into tufted cords to create a fabric of great depth and richness. Aptly named after the French word for "caterpillar", this luxuriously furry material is used to make blankets, throws, and furniture upholstery.

Cotton is a lightweight fabric woven from spun fibres from the boll of the cotton plant. Breathable, washable, and endlessly versatile, it's the perfect all-season fabric for bedding, upholstery, and window coverings. Long-staple or Egyptian cottons are the softest options for bedding, while sun-treated canvas and twills are durable choices for outdoor furnishings. Cotton is often blended with linen, wool, silk, or synthetic fibres.

raw linen

twill

sisal rug

kilim rug

Denim is a heavy, twill-woven cotton fabric that is believed to have originated in France and was popularized in the US during the California Gold Rush in the form of work trousers (jeans). Denim is a great washable loose-cover option for casual rooms, especially where children and pets play, as well as outdoor rooms. Repeated washings soften the fabric, adding to its appeal.

Faux suede is designed to mimic the look and touch of genuine napped leather. Made of microfibres, this durable synthetic offers a soft, washable upholstery option for sofas and chairs and contributes a lush feeling to rooms.

Leather makes an exceptionally durable upholstery option that gets more supple and beautiful with age. The surface texture, dimension, pigment regularity, and softness of the tanned hide all distinguish high-quality leather. Black and brown are classic leather colours, but manufacturers now dye leathers in a range of attractive hues. Leather furnishings suit both contemporary and classic interiors.

Linen *(pictured above)* is woven from the fibres of the flax plant. Twice as strong as cotton, this crisp, breathable fabric has a naturally nubby texture that softens with use. Linen is a popular choice for tablecloths and napkins, curtains, and upholstery. It is often blended with cotton for easier care. Machine-washable linen is now widely available.

Matelassé *(pictured above)* is a double-woven fabric, usually of cotton, with raised decorative patterns that mimic the look of a quilt (*matelassé* means "cushioned" in French). In fact, the effect is achieved through the process

of weaving in an interlocking wadding weft (a filled thread or yarn) rather than through quilting. Matelassé bedding, cushions, and throws lend rich texture and vintage appeal to a room.

Silk is woven from threads unwound from cocoons of the Japanese silkworm. Prized for its beautiful sheen and smooth texture, silk is a luxurious option for curtains and pillow coverings.

Synthetic fibres such as rayon, polyester, nylon, and acrylic are woven into a wide range of natural fabrics to make them more durable and easier to maintain.

Terry cloth, the classic towelling fabric, is usually woven of cotton and has a looped surface that is naturally absorbent. Because it washes well, dries fast, and withstands humidity, terry makes an ideal upholstery fabric or cushion covering for bathrooms and outdoor spaces.

Twill *(pictured above)* is a cotton fabric that is tightly woven with a raised diagonal grain. Denim and gabardine are examples of twill weaves. Durable, washable, and comfortable, cotton twill is a hardworking choice for loose covers or upholstery, indoors and out. Sun-treated twills stand up to outdoor use best.

Velvet is traditionally woven from wool, silk, or cotton. Its raised pile consists of rows of loops that are cut to produce a plush, fur-like texture. A classic choice for curtains and upholstery, velvet brings a rich and elegant accent to interiors.

Wool makes a naturally strong, warm, and resilient fabric for home furnishings. Wool fibres are commonly blended with natural fibres or synthetics.

Rugs

Abaca, also called Manila hemp, is an extremely strong fibre that comes from the leafstalk of a banana plant that is native to the Philippines. Abaca is not related to true hemp, although both are used to make twine, fabric, and rugs.

Coir is a natural fibre derived from coconut husks. Once removed from the husks, the fibre is spun and machine woven into matting. Coir mats have a coarse finish and are generally considered the toughest of the natural-fibre rugs. Coir is a good option for hallways and is widely used for doormats.

Cotton yarns are woven to make rugs that feel soft and springy underfoot, with the added advantage of being easy to clean. Styles range from the tapestry-weave dhurries of India to American designs such as braided rugs and rag rugs. Naturally absorbent, cotton mats are the rug of choice for bathrooms.

Jute comes from a strong, woody plant grown extensively in Asia. When woven into matting, it has a lush appearance and texture akin to wool. Jute is considered the softest underfoot of the natural woven mats, but in general does not prove as long-wearing as sisal or seagrass.

Paper rugs are woven from fibres extracted from wood pulp. Surprisingly durable and comfortable underfoot, paper rugs are woven in attractive patterns that have the look of sisal and other natural matting. They are an environmentally sound option, as wood is recyclable and biodegradable.

Seagrass is a commercially grown aquatic grass from China that produces a fibre similar to straw and smoother than coir, sisal, or jute. It is naturally resistant to dirt and stains, making it suitable for higher-traffic areas. The subtle green tones of seagrass (which eventually soften to brown) add warmth and outdoor appeal to a room.

Sisal *(pictured above)* is a flexible fibre made from the leaves of the sisal (or agave) plant, which grows in Asia, Africa, and Central America. Sisal fibres are woven into hardwearing rugs with an even, highly textural surface. They are relatively soft, making them a fine choice for living areas and bedrooms. Their durability also makes them suitable for hallways.

Synthetic rugs – machine-woven from fibres such as nylon, rayon, polyester, or acrylic – are durable, stain resistant, and affordable. Polypropylene is a petroleum-based synthetic that can be woven into striking patterns that look like natural sisal or wool. Easy to clean with water, polypropylene rugs are a practical choice in high-traffic rooms such as halls and kitchens and in outdoor areas.

Wool rugs are naturally warm, water repellent, and long-lasting. Most wool carpets are woven with synthetic fibres, typically in a blend of 80 per cent wool, 20 per cent nylon. Wool yarns are additionally used to weave intricately patterned Oriental and Tibetan rugs as well as the kilims of Turkey and Afghanistan *(pictured above)*.

Index